Blogs Change Lives

A practical, inspirational guide to building a blog that could change your life.

Aby Moore

To my daughter Ava.

You can do anything you want,

You can achieve anything you set your mind to,

You can create a life you love by building your own empire.

'She believed she could, so she did'

R. S. Grey

'OMG - I've just finished your book and to say I love it is an understatement! I cried in the first chapter and smiled with delight in the last chapter, seriously it's brilliant!!'
Cherry

'Jam-packed with 'Aby's Action Steps' and brilliant motivational quotes, 'Blogs Change Lives' is the ONLY blogging book you'll need to start and grow a successful online blogging business!' Kelly

'I am genuinely blown away by how fab it is! Definitely an unputdownable book!'
Cherry

Contents

'Turning your passion into your job is easier than finding a job that matches your passion'

Seth Godin

Sharing my daughter's story started my own.

I sat in the bathroom and leant my head against the wall. Silent tears streamed down my face. Those tears had become regulars on my cheeks over the last few weeks. That fact alone made me feel so guilty. Guilty for having everything I had been dreaming of for so long, yet still feeling so sad and empty. Guilty for having a beautiful baby girl who was so wanted yet being unable to stop crying. I had everything I knew so many women still wanted, yet I was sitting there, my head on the wall with the tears making their seventh appearance of the day. I could hear my hubby and sister-in-law in the living room. Two of the people I loved most in the world, but their presence and support didn't make me feel any less alone. Maybe I was broken?

I had never imagined that trying to fall pregnant would be so overwhelming, all-consuming and utterly heart-breaking. The experience of being poked, tested, prodded and then told they had no idea why we hadn't got our baby yet was soul destroying. For me, the visual representation of the dream I had was the pregnancy wallet the midwife gives you when you have successfully created a baby. An outward sign to the world that you were about to become a lucky member of that exclusive 'mum' club. I started to believe that I would never hold that wallet in my hands; I would never be someone's mum. I had even started looking at adoption online as I knew I HAD to be a mum, but I so desperately wanted a child that was ours.

On 9th August 2012, I was staggered to find out that I was pregnant. Even though I celebrated, my heart felt convinced that something would go wrong. After all, why would it have worked now? Why would it work for us the month before our first IVF consultation? Every trip to the toilet for those nine long months was terrifying. Would I see blood, at times I even convinced myself I could? I wasn't sure I was strong enough to lose a second baby.

After three months on crutches due to a failing pelvis, Ava was induced on her due date. Fourteen hours into labour they pressed the red button to request the emergency medical team. Despite the pain and sheer terror I was feeling, I remember turning to my husband and saying, 'I told you something was going to go wrong'. Even then, minutes away from meeting our baby girl, I was convinced she would be taken from me.

Fast forward seven months and it was a total surprise to me when the doctor told me I was suffering from post natal depression. How could I be? I wasn't that type of person... I was a go-getter who just, well, got on with things. Sadly, those low, empty feelings had come once too often, prompting a visit to my doctor. She told me it was a chemical imbalance and could affect anyone. It was nothing I had done. It was just like any other illness. I walked home thinking how it shouldn't have affected me; I didn't have the right to feel depressed. I had my little girl.

'Get out of the house every day' a friend's words were stuck fast in my head. So I did. I diligently went to local baby groups and on almost all occasions, I'd have paid money to be able to stay at home. I ventured out nevertheless. At times these groups were so difficult. Trying to make chit-chat with strangers, when all I wanted was to be lying in bed, was draining to say the least.

You see, before I became a mum I had a job I loved. I was great at it and I had a wonderful social circle around me. I didn't expect that introducing a baby into the mix would cause some of these 'friends' to visit once then never contact me again or even worse just never engage with me at all. They never even got to meet my beautiful daughter. Now I realise that is totally their loss, but it still hurts to this day.

It turns out that sometimes your body can react badly to a difficult birth, losing your identity, your job and then pretty much all your friends, in a matter of months. People said it wasn't surprising after all I'd been through. It still surprised me though. I just couldn't get my head around the label I had been given.

Over the weeks that followed I had at times, overwhelming feelings of extreme loneliness, even when I was sitting in a room full of people. Like I was a fly on the wall of my own life.

Fast forward four years, I'm sat on the Eurostar on my way home having attended entrepreneurial conference mixing with seven figure business owners. My head is as full as my heart. The landscape of my life is a far cry from how it looked four years ago. I've changed too and I'm unrecognisable from that girl who sat with her head against the wall and the tears free-flowing down her face and splashing onto the floor.

What changed in my life? I started a blog.

A blog that changed my life.

CHAPTER 1

Small acorns and big dreams.

What I didn't know when I typed those first few words pretty much on a whim was just how powerful that would be. How amazing the world was that I was about to enter. How the friends I would go on to make would be the very best of friends, better than I ever thought I would have. I didn't know, just by starting this blog that my life would totally and unequivocally be changed forever.

August 2013

Ava was four and a half months old and I was pretty convinced I wasn't going to win any mum of the year awards anytime soon. I was so sure I would forget the milestones; that first smile, the first time she rolled over. When was it that she took her first step?

In my head, forgetting one of these facts would relegate me to the bad-mummy list. I felt compelled to try to create a rich history for her. I wanted to document our lives so she would have lots of information and context around her childhood. It would show her that she was always so loved, it would show her our smiles, our happy lives and it would be something special; my gift to her.

I spent hours upon hours stranded on the couch under my gorgeous sleeping child. I could only move my right arm. So one afternoon on 15th August 2013 I picked up my laptop and I googled 'how to start a blog'. No-one would ever read it, I mean why would they? That wasn't important, or even a consideration for me at the time. I had no desire to be famous or to gain online notoriety. It would simply be a way I could diarise moments, thoughts and events that happened in our lives. No-one would read it I thought, but Ava would have it and she would know how much she was loved every single moment of her life.

It would be our little space online to show her complete story. I took all my Ava related Facebook updates and moments that had been etched on my mind and put them on my blog, right back to the day I found out I was pregnant. I wanted her story to start right at the beginning.

It started slowly, I would write about things that cropped up during our day to day lives. Not confident enough to be bold with my writing but enjoying it nevertheless. About three times a week, I would post updates on my blog. Sharing our lives, my thoughts, and I remember being quite surprised that I had about thirty-five daily readers. Thirty-five people that I didn't know. I knew I didn't know them at first because I hadn't told anyone I had a blog.

While reading more and more blogs, I realised they were like reading a never-ending novel. Have you ever read a book and got so invested in the story of the characters' lives that you feel sadness, even slightly bereft, when the book ends? Well, with blogs, I got all the benefits of reading a novel, but the end never came. I could carry on enjoying learning about these other women online, who were sharing their families with the world too, just as I was. I was hooked.

Being quite an all-in kind of girl, it wasn't long before I wanted to know everything about this intriguing online world that I'd stumbled into. There seemed so much possibility and the more I learned, the more I wanted to learn.

As time went on, my love for my blog and the community grew. I met new people; new friends. Time and time again I was blown away by their talent, the support they offered and their kindness. People with similar lives and goals coming together over their desire to share their own story in their own voice.

We all have a voice, we just have to know how to use it.

As my confidence grew, so did my skills and I strengthened my voice. I became less afraid to publish my words and more immersed in the community. People who I met online became friends that I would speak to everyday. Right there is the proof of the power of blogging at its finest. To this day, most of my best friends in this world are people I've met online.

My own therapy

My blog was merely a modern-day baby book at the start. There was no grand plan; no thoughts of world domination. Just a broken mum recording her life to try and fill a hole which had appeared. As I began committing our memories to the screen, I started to benefit in more ways than I ever would have dreamed of. For me, the process of writing is cathartic, like therapy; it helps me in so many ways. It did way back then and it still does to this day.

See, I stupidly never thought that it would happen to me. That I would never *get* depression. I'm a problem-solving, get up and go kind of person; a 'Do-er'. Plus, I'd finally got my little girl, everything I'd wanted for many years, how could I be depressed? I soon realised depression is something that you have no control over. Whether it's a chemical imbalance or your reaction to that imbalance, it's certainly isn't a matter of choice or character. Things that you normally can do become a struggle. Your confidence is low and silly things can cause you so much stress and anxiety. You can be in such a happy setting, such as an amazing family day out surrounded by the people you love the most in the world, yet a feeling of incredible sadness and disconnection washes over you.

Like many other mums, having a baby was the best thing to happen to me. However, since having a baby, there was such a huge chunk of time when I didn't feel like *me* anymore. For the most part, I'm fine with that, people change. Physically and mentally I'm so far away from the person I was before. I just wanted to recognise myself a little bit more and writing my blog helped me to get me back. It encouraged me to look for the silver lining and to focus on the positive things in each and every day. Not to romanticise about my life, but to try to focus on the positives - of which there were many. I can still cry when I have a really lovely day, but that's just how it is. I'm not sure how long those feelings will stay with me, maybe forever. However, for the most part, I'm a million miles from where I was.

Without my blog, the nice moments and happy times would be far less frequent. My blog is helping to build my confidence and my self-esteem EVERY DAY, even to this day. Through my blog, I'm part of a community of like-minded supportive people, where previously I felt isolated. It's amazing how many 'friends' no longer bother calling when you have a baby. My blog has given me a sense of pride and accomplishment, my own corner of the internet. It's given me back self-worth.

We should get to know each other, shouldn't we?

I'm guessing from the fact that you're reading this book, that you're at least a little bit interested in having your life changed? You might be curious about the power of blogging or just like me at the start, you want somewhere to store all those special memories. Either way, you've come to the right place. I'm going to take you on an adventure from the start of my blogging life to the point I sat down to write this book. You will see how I turned my ~~hobby~~ passion into a business and I'll share with you my practical advice so you can do it too! Deal? Great, let's get started!

Those first few posts

Have you ever pressed publish on a post and wondered whether anyone would read it? Would those who do read it actually care? What will it take to make your blog stand out? How will you create content that will make people remember you and help you start to create relationships with your readers?

It can be really hard when you create posts, especially those which you know will help others, when you don't get the readers you hoped for. Sometimes our *best* posts just don't seem to get traction. When this happens, do you worry that your writing is not good enough? Maybe all the other bloggers out there are more talented? Why do they all seem to get traffic and you don't? What are they offering their readers that you aren't? I would guess they are giving more of themselves. They are letting their readers into their lives and they are making them *feel* something.

You know what you have to do right? You have to share your story. More of YOU.

Your story is so powerful

In fact, it's the most powerful thing we have in our online businesses. Words have the power to inspire, to motivate, to evoke emotion and move people to action, to creativity, to achieve great things. Words can also entertain and make people feel connected to each other.

Stories are such an important factor in human communication. We have a need to hear stories and to close the psychological loop they open in our minds before we can move on. This is why sometimes it's hard to put a book down. Our desire to close the psychological loop and 'see what happens' leaves us always want to read a story to the end. Have you ever skipped to the last page of a book you were reading? Yes, me too! We were too impatient to wait for the writer to close the psychological loop.

"The universe is made of stories, not of atoms" - Muriel Rukeyser

Stories give people the chance to experience, albeit second-hand, so many new experiences. Stories, if told well, can evoke those feelings of 'I've been there' in others, which will strengthen the bond between the person telling the story and those reading it. Stories give information much more context and meaning. These reasons and more make sharing your story so important.

This is how you become unforgettable as a blogger

Stories allow us to connect in a much deeper way with our readers meaning that blog posts using stories will be much more memorable than those which just simply give facts.

For your message to be heard and be retained by your readers, sharing stories around your information is vital. We're all busy and we read so much content online each and every day. If we're honest we probably forget most of it by the time our kids have thrown their 20th daily tantrum and we've laid our heads on our pillows at night. What we do remember, however, is the stories we identified with. Your stories make you memorable and they make your audience connect with you.

It's human nature to like people who entertain us and most of us read for entertainment. If you tell stories, your posts become more than just words, they will become entertainment too. They won't all be funny; some will be heart-warming or dramatic, but they will entertain.

People love reading content that's funny, heartfelt, surprising, motivating. Content with emotions and stories weaved into it. Your stories will create a picture of a future situation that the reader will become invested in. Then you can use a call to action to inspire them to follow through and take the desired action.

Stories can be a remarkable way to show your vulnerability. The vulnerable parts of your life make you even more relatable and real to your readers. Your readers will resonate with you much more if you share the *real* you. So, show up and expose your vulnerability.

Stories can be like testimonials. They help you illustrate a point and make content more meaningful and consequently more memorable. You can use stories in any blog and with every topic you write about. No topic is too abstract for a story, there will always be a way to make this story relatable to your readers.

Now you know that you need to incorporate stories into your content, where do you find your stories? How do you find that fabulous story that will bring your post to life?

Our lives are made up of millions of experiences. They're not all earth shattering, granted, but they are all stories which help to share more of you with your audience. Pick a story which sums up the point you are trying to make with your content or a story which could lead nicely into the main theme of your content.

These stories don't all have to be your personal experiences. Yes, it's great if some of them are, but you can use stories from your audience, clients, family or even from research. You know what? You can even make up a story to illustrate a point and if it's well written, it will still have the desired effect (always be transparent with your readers if you do this!).

The power of telling your story means that you will be able to reach your audience in a way which will make them want to come back to read more and more. To invest their time in you. Whether we believe it or not our own story can and will inspire others, so that story needs to be told.

Your audience needs it. **Your audience needs you.**

ABY'S ACTION STEP

I want you to start a 'Stories Swipe file'. Often we forget those little moments in our lives that can be retold in the future. This little moment can be impactful and help you illustrate your point, giving depth to your content.

Your first challenge is to pick up a pretty notebook — I know you have PLENTY of them lying around! — and start to record stories from your life and those around you which illustrate main concepts. This might be a moment when you believed in yourself. Or a time you felt validated. Keep these stories pertinent to your content or your personal journey.

This record will commit these stories to memory and you will realise the power they have. Then when you need to add depth to content you are writing you have this ready-made swipe file. So grab a notebook and start adding your stories.

CHAPTER 2

A question of clarity.

When I began blogging, I knew I wanted to preserve our special family memories. I was totally compelled to keep on documenting week after week. Over the years, the clarity I have around my blog (and now my business) has changed focus. I'm still, however, just as clear as I was during those first few months.

You know it's okay if you start something and then change your mind on where your passions lie. That's life. **Never be afraid of leaping**. Give yourself permission to try different things on for size and your superpower will unveil itself to you, believe me, mine did.

As my journey progressed and writing became my job, it became easier and easier to press the publish button without the worrying about being judged. You see, your opinion matters, your opinion is what makes you unique, it's your USP (unique selling point). If you sit on the fence, despite the splinters you may get in your bum, you're not giving anyone a reason to read your story. So, while I'll never be the most controversial blogger, I will never shy away from sharing my opinion. I will never be fearful about whether I have the right to have that opinion. We **ALL** have that right. Your opinion is just as valid as anyone else's, don't forget that.

You see, fear can be at best an annoyance, and at worst crippling. A natural instinct that can affect your life in so many ways if you let it. I always think it's better to be remembered for the wonderful things about your personality, not for the most basic of instincts that we all possess.

People will always judge; rather they judge you on having an opinion and not agreeing with you, than of being devoid of any conviction at all.

Your writing is your opportunity to share your story. People want to listen, so share something worth listening to.

Back to my own story

It hadn't taken long for me to be hooked on blogging and so in January 2014 I took the leap and moved my site to self-hosted WordPress. This meant I could have more control over how the site looked. I cobbled together a header of pictures of Ava, hoping that it would give a glimpse of what we were about as a family. Looking back now I cringe so much, but it was an honest start and it was *my* start. I had no idea what I was doing, but I knew I wanted to show more of us and images seemed to be the way to go.

As I got more and more involved in blogging, I knew I would need to create a more professional header. It wasn't long before I commissioned the wonderful Helen Braid to draw a bespoke header. I loved it and felt that with this design my blog really developed and came into its own. I started to secure more work and my stats grew and grew. I rose up the rankings and each time this happened

I remained amazed that people were actually reading my little piece of the internet. Amazed, but so happy that they were. A sentiment that I still feel to this day.

Having a cohesive brand is so important.

"A brand is a name, term, design, symbol, or any other feature that identifies one seller's goods or services as distinct from those of other sellers" (American Marketing Association).

There's a lot of talk online about branding. Once branding was considered a business logo and that was pretty much it. In today's business world, branding is a whole lot more. Branding is everything you say and do online, even the image people have of you and your company is related to branding.

"Your brand is what other people say about you when you're not in the room." – Jeff Bezos

Think of the golden arches (McDonalds). You know what those arches signify; you know what the restaurant will look like. You know how the staff will be dressed and you're clear the food that will be on offer. You have an expectation because you are familiar with the McDonalds brand.

Obviously, through your branding, you want your ideal reader/customer to see you as the best choice over your competition. However, ideally you want your branding to make you feel like you are the only sensible choice. The only option for them.

Great branding will:

- Improve your credibility.
- Create an emotional connection between your audience and you/your product.
- Make your audience want to buy into your brand.
- Help you project your message.

I know what you're thinking. Well, that all sounds great, but where do you start?

The first step is to be really familiar with your audience's needs, desires and pain points.

Great branding crosses the line between what represents you as the business owner and what will resonate with your ideal audience. If you get it right, your branding will reflect you and your message, while also being exactly what your ideal readers are looking for.

Don't forget consistency is key here.

Consistent branding will lead to more confidence from your audience. Creating a consistent look and feel to every part of your brand online takes real effort, but the importance should not be underestimated. Ideally, you want people to see an image, part of a logo or even your colour palette and instantly connect it to your brand.

Create a blog style guide and stick to it.

A style guide details all the aspects that feed into your branding. Creating one single document that you can then refer back to every time you create content makes sure you stay on brand.

This style guide will include your colour palette, font choices, graphics elements, how you write certain words, whether you capitalise headers and such. When you have this style guide refer back to it regularly.

OK. so you've created this guide, what's next?

Take time to examine your current branding. Are your audience connecting with your brand? Which aspects seem a good fit? Does your current branding sum up what you're about and what you offer your audience? Consider new audience members, will they be able to understand what your brand is about from their first impressions?

If you feel unsure about any of these questions, then this is should be what you focus first.

Aspects of branding

Your blog/business name

Names are so important. Some of us name our blog/business and then feel a bit stuck with it. In reality, it's never too late to change. There just might be some negative aspects (such as a drop in Domain Authority), but this won't last forever. Ideally, your name should reflect what your blog is about, so people landing on your site know immediately what content to expect. A name which accurately sums up your content will also help you in search engine rankings.

Your website URL

Carefully select your URL. Having the structure as close as possible to your blog name is really important. Personally, I think .com is preferable. Unless you are focusing on the UK market or are for a specific UK area, such as my awesome friend Ceri from thiswelshmother.co.uk. It just makes sense for Ceri's URL to be .co.uk. Sometimes, you might find that both .co.uk and .com are not available. In this case, I would go for .co, which is becoming increasingly popular with many reputable sites. For me, .net and other variations don't seem professional.

Logo

Your logo could be professionally designed by a third party or knocked-up yourself in Canva, there's no judgement here! It could have graphics elements or simple typography, but it must 'fit' with your brand's ethos. In most cases, less is more.

Blog tagline

A tagline can give immediate context and it can help you to clarify who you're writing for and what your content will be about. It can also add personality. Taglines can also be handy to help your readers when your blog name isn't 100% on the brand.

Using my main brand as an example, You Baby Me Mummy. I started my blog literally as a memory book online, so the name didn't matter to me. Over the years my blog has grown and its focus has grown and shifted to content about blogging and being a mamapreneur, which doesn't naturally 'fit' with my blog name. However, the site has great authority and in 2017 hit number one in the Tots100 rankings (for UK parenting blogs) for the first time. It also has a Domain Authority of around fifty depending on the month. Therefore, to change name and URL would be costly.

This is where my tagline can be used to help those people who do land on my site. 'Leading the Mamapreneur Revolution' gives a glimpse of what my blog is about and ties this brand into my second brand The Mamapreneur

Revolution. So, while it's not the ideal situation, it's a good enough solution.

Header

The header is the combination of your logo and tagline. It's such an important aspect of your blog. Being the first thing people will see when they land on your site, it needs to be right. It needs to show your personality and give a hint of what you're about. While remaining professional and not too clip-arty! Don't clutter your header — prioritise clarity. Also, make sure your header isn't too deep as it will then take up all the space above the fold (the space that is visible on the screen before the reader scrolls).

Theme

Your theme is an important part of your blog and so you should make sure the one you choose is right for your needs — not just the one everyone else seems to be using! The right theme will allow you to present your content in a way that makes sense and will have an effect on the reader's experience, so it's worth getting this right.

You should also bear in mind how bulky the theme is. The more bells and whistles it has, the higher the chances are that it could slow down your blog.

Themes can also be made to look very different, with colour schemes, fonts, layout choices, and images. A great tip when you're thinking of purchasing a theme is to head over to Pinterest and just search the name of the theme. This will give you lots of different customisations that people have created and so you'll have a better idea of the options before you jump in and buy one.

Also, think about what's important to you to show off on your blog. Are you a photographer who needs your images to be laid out beautifully or do you run events and would need some sort of diary system on your site? Whatever your 'thing' is, make sure the theme you pick is perfect for the main characteristic of your site.

Voice

I've spoken about how important it is to find your voice and then to use it. Your ideal reader needs to hear you and will only resonate with the real you if you use your own voice! *Your* voice is so powerful and is the factor that will set you apart from everyone else out there because **no-one** is *you.*

Fonts

The most important question to ask when selecting the fonts for your site is, are they legible? You may choose a serif font (with the little feet on the letters) or a more modern sans serif. The choice is yours. You can also obviously mix the two types of fonts. Selecting one-three fonts that complement each other will mean that you have options for body text and different sized headers.

Colours

The colours you pick need to be consistent and again represent the image you wish to project. Choose between three and five colours that work together. You won't use all of them in everything you create, but you can use them when necessary. Even if it's just to use as an accent colour. coolors.co is an awesome site which makes finding colours palettes really easy and fun!

Patterns

If you love leopard print then you can use this as an occasional accent, but make sure you choose a pattern to reflect your aesthetic.

Photographs

All your photographs should have the same style and in a perfect world the same edit. This isn't always possible as we learn as we go, and our style evolves. However, it's what we should be aiming for. We don't want someone to read a current post and then click to an older post and wonder if they're still on the same site. Consistency is key. Your photos should be as wide as your theme allows, not stuck in the middle of the page.

Graphics

Your graphics should be consistent too and stay on brand. If you're creating an elegant and professional brand and then randomly drop a gif in a post, it will stick out like a sore thumb. Any social media graphics should be consistent and reflect your branding.

Your language

Do you write in a really relaxed manner or are you more professional in the way you communicate? Which words do you often use in real life? Keep a note of these to include in your copy. This language needs to be kept consistent across all your social media platforms and communication in general.

Design

Beautiful, stylish design can make such a difference to your blog. Like it or not, even the best writing can be overlooked in a sea of bright colours and poorly selected fonts. There's a saying that we 'eat with our eyes first' and I think that goes for blogs too. You consume the blog with your eyes first and then begin to read, if you're not put off that is.

My blog has changed so much since I published my first post and most of the designs I have done myself, so I know you can too.

Do your research. Look at lots of blogs, decide what you like about them and what you don't like as much. Look at your own blog and identify the bits that don't make you happy anymore. Do you like someone else's sidebar layout? What about their author bio box? Or the font they use? By using them as inspiration you are not copying, you're just narrowing down what you want and getting your creative juices flowing. If you're a visual person sketch out your ideas and see how they fit together.

Remember, your theme must work for you. You can buy themes from many places and some design subscriptions even give them away in their newsletters. Have a look at Creative Market, Etsy and Theme Forest, who all offer a great range of themes for around £20-£70. Make sure the theme functions how you want it to. How many menus do you need? Do you want a slider image?

Check that when people land on your blog they're going to get a feel of you, your family and your personality. Does the theme allow you to make it clear straight away what your content will be?

Are you happy with the background that comes with your theme? Do you want to leave it plain white? You can get your header illustrated, use photographs or just stick to text. Illustrated characters can date your design, which means you will need to redo your header as your family grows. This might not be an issue, but it's something to bear in mind. When your design is finished, you will need to do resized versions for all your social media platforms and your email signature.

Don't forget to create a Favicon. This is the little image or letter that appears on the blog or website name in the top tab, for example the Pinterest one is the white P in the red circle. You will need to change this from the generic theme one. Just find a small section of your design which represents your blog or the initials and creates a small image to drop into the favicon section of your customiser.

Even if it's just in a Word document, write down all the style information for your blog. For example, which fonts have you used? What sizes? What are the hex codes of the various colours? Having this information together in one place will make the customising task much easier.

Before you make your new theme live, you can customise some of it. Have a play around and see what you can amend in the preview mode, this will leave you less to do when you hit publish. Try to publish your new theme when you think your blog traffic will be low, so that you have some time to quickly drop things over and adjust colours before anyone notices.

If you think all this is a little out of your comfort zone, there are many companies that offer stylish web design and calling in the professionals would certainly be an investment, especially if your techie skills are a bit rusty.

ABY'S ACTION STEP

Whether you have a blog or not I want you to create a style guide. You can research using a secret Pinterest board. Pin everything you like and then extract the elements you want to go into your branding. You will need the HEX codes of the colours you wish to use, the names of the fonts, any patterns, sizes of headers. Try to document everything, so you will be able to keep your branding consistent.

CHAPTER 3

How to make your posts rock.

Post layout

Post layout is an important part of the design of your blog. This must remain consistent too. Document how you're going to lay posts out. Which headers will you include? How many pictures will you include? If you include a video where will it go? Will your pin be positioned at the bottom or half way through?

Your post formatting should be consistent

Have you ever landed on a blog and bounced straight back off it again? I have… Do you know what makes that happen more often than not? It's not because the reader has read some content that they disagree with or didn't like. It's not because they can't resonate with what you message. Nope, they're not there long enough to even read anything.

They bounce because they don't like the way it looks. How superficial you might say! The fact of the matter is in a world with millions of blogs and websites, appearances matter. This is true for your blog design, but also for your actual individual posts.

If the reader makes it past the homepage of your blog, but lands on a page which is hard to read or is unappealing, I'll happily bet money on the fact that they'll not be hanging around long. Today's blog readers are spoilt for choice and they don't want to work hard for their information.

This is why formatting your blog posts properly is so important. So, simple yet so overlooked. Making sure your posts are easy to consume is such an important step. Many bloggers miss the important factors when it comes to formatting blog posts. Making your posts easy to read, means that the traffic you do get will stick around and they will probably even come back.

As humans, we're a little lazy and very busy. Consequently, we want to consume information quickly so we can move on. Making your content easy to skim read will make your readers love you. Therefore learning how to format a blog post becomes really important. You might have crafted a masterpiece, but the truth is that readers on average will only read about 20% of the text on a webpage so you need to make sure they can see your golden nuggets!

Use images/photos

Humans process images 60,000 times faster than text. Yep, 60,000 times! Crazy isn't it?! Nothing makes me sadder than when I click on a post and it's like War and Peace laid out in front of me. The wall of text is so overwhelming. It's your job not to overwhelm your readers, but to take them through your content and give them a pleasant experience. Use images and/or photos, with any other visuals (think video, infographics and even GIFs!) to break up the text and punctuate your message.

Use lists if they work for the post

People LOVE a list. They're so easy to consume, mega skimmable and perfect to use in blog posts. People want fast content and lists give them that very thing. The most skimmable content format alive is a list, so make good use of them if it fits your particular topic.

Keep your paragraphs short and punchy

Try using a maximum of two or three sentences per paragraph. The extra white space around your text gives it space to breathe (and the reader too). White space gives a confident and professional appearance to your layout and it will be appreciated by your audience.

Consider using an infographic

If your post includes fact and figures, then why not create an infographic. These are super sharable and help people process the information, as well as helping to break up the text.

I created a few infographics and used them as the post pins and they've been really popular. If you haven't got a design eye, don't worry you can find lots of templates in Canva, that are pretty much done for you.

Use headings and subheadings properly

To punctuate the lovely short-paragraph and white-space layout you now have, you should use headings. This breaks the content up into sections and adds to the positive reading experience.

If you include your keywords in these headings you will also be improving your SEO too! Try to use H1 and H2 tags. The H1 tag is your blog post title and the headings within your post are H2s. Then, as you work through your post include H3 and H4 headings.

In WordPress, just click on the **Paragraph** drop down to see your available options.

Use bold on the important words (like your keywords!)

Using **bold text** really helps your reader **skim down** the page and highlights the parts of the text they should pay attention to. Don't go crazy but use bold where appropriate to help your readers.

Whether you're writing a short and sweet 500-word post or an epic 2-4k word one you need to bear these factors in mind to make sure your readers can get to the end of your post.

As you can see 'branding' includes so many factors. However, by nailing these areas and by creating a style guide to keep you on track. You will be able to maintain this consistency and you will be creating an epic stand-out brand.

Let's dig in a bit more to actually constructing your posts

Having a good structure to your content ensures that people will be able to read and understand your content more easily. Having a way to structure the *creation* of your content makes life easier for you too and we ALL want an easy life!

Fancy creating a post step by step?

The first step is to plan your post. Choose the topic, do your research, find your angle and gather the information from any sources or stats you might want to reference. Use Google search and a keyword planner to decide on the best keywords for the post. Then outline your post making note of your key points in each section.

Next, create a headline that's informative and that will also capture readers' attention. Headlines can make or break a post. The perfect headline is one which explains what the person will get from reading the post, as well as

• 33 •

piquing their interest. Odd numbers are said to be psychologically more attractive to people than even ones, so if relevant, it would be good to include them. The ideal structure is:

Odd number + Superlative + Exact keyword phrase

(7 + Amazing + Wordpress Plugins for Bloggers)

Now get to work writing your post. Whether you choose to work in sections or write the entire post in one sitting, it's up to you. The key here is just to write. Don't edit as you go and if you make a mistake just keep writing. Ideally thinking about incorporating your chosen keyword/keyword phrase where you can.

When you have your draft ready, it's time to channel your inner tech geek and think about Search Engine Optimisation (SEO). Make sure you've optimised the post to the best of your ability. Yoast (a WP plugin) is a good call as this really spells out what you need to do to your post to improve the optimisation.

Next up are the images. Adding images will enhance your post and make it much more appealing to your readers. Images improve a posts flow, they can explain complex topics more easily and can they can even add humour. Research shows that content with visuals gets 94% more views (Forbes).

It's a great idea to create four separate images for a post on top of those you use to describe your content. You will need to create a featured image for your actual blog post — a Pinterest pin, a Facebook sized image, and a Twitter optimised graphic too. Posts get more reach if the images are optimised to the recommended size for each platform.

Editing time! This is my least favourite part of the entire process. However, it's so important to edit your posts to avoid repetition and eliminate typos or grammatical errors. A great way to edit is to read your post aloud to check its flow.

If possible, you could ask someone else read it and provide feedback. Over the years my hubby has read countless posts of mine to give them a once over. Remember in the edit to keep sentences and paragraphs short. Don't be a perfectionist and don't be afraid to cut out text or adapt your writing at the last minute. You can also check that the headings are descriptive and are using the proper sizes as we discussed earlier (H2, H3 etc). Make sure you have added the relevant internal and external links. Cut down super long blocks of copy and add formatting such as bold, italics, bulleted lists etc. Then give it a final proofread.

Now, comes the part a lot of people gloss over —the promotion. You need to have a system for promoting your posts and for getting them out into the world. If you haven't got a set promotion schedule it's likely that you will forget to promote your posts on some platforms during your busy day.

Here's an example promotion schedule:

Share once on Facebook on the day the post is live. You might want to reword this post and schedule it again for a few weeks in advance (as long as it's evergreen in nature). While you're over here on Facebook, you can share the post in any relevant groups that allow sharing.

Then go over to Twitter. I share each new post every ten hours for twenty insertions. When this sequence is completed and as long as the post is evergreen, I schedule it to tweet once every thirty hours forever.

If your post is helpful in nature you should definitely pin it to Pinterest. Pin it to your blog board, all of your other relevant boards, then share to group boards and Tribes too.

You might then choose to add it to Stumbleupon or promote it using Instagram.

If you're looking for ways to maximise your traffic, consider teasing the post on Facebook live or Instagram Live/Stories.

Now you know how to write the perfect post and have a plan to promote it, but how do you plan content month by month so you can create this magic over and over again?

I used to write over sixty posts a month, yes 6 0! In fact, in one month clocked in at eighty-three posts! Madness! Now, there's no way you have to post that frequently, nowhere near in fact. One thing you do need to do in order to grow your blog is to **plan your content** so you can be consistent. This tells Google that you're updating your site regularly (which will help you in terms of search engine rankings). It also gives your readers a reason to come back to your blog. I'm going to walk you through how I have learned to plan my content over the years and I've planned A LOT of content!

Time to organise your content

I'm one of life's planners. I like to be organised and don't like the feeling of being out of control. There are many different types of bloggers. Some people prefer to fly by the seat of their pants, publishing as and when they want, writing the night before the deadline and they seem to thrive like this. I, however, do not. I like to be organised, know where I'm going and if possible have a plan to get me there too. Things are much more predictable that way.

I think that having an editorial calendar is so important to your blog's success. First, I want to mention that an editorial calendar can take many different forms, depending on how you like to work. It could be a simple diary, an Excel spreadsheet, chart, or as I have, an editorial calendar WordPress plugin.

In essence, an editorial calendar is a tool that keeps you, as a blogger, a season ahead. This is vital, as you need to be aware and be able to plan for events, seasons, trends and holidays. Most pro bloggers will prepare well in advance for such notable dates. Your calendar allows you the opportunity to get ahead, be consistent and gain momentum, which will all help to drive traffic to your blog.

Personally, the main benefit of using an editorial calendar is to get a visual picture of my content month by month. This allows for better planning for seasonal opportunities. You don't start thinking about Christmas posts in December, you need to start planning them around September time or even earlier.

Planning your content also helps you develop consistency, which readers love. People like to know when your new posts will be live. Having an editorial calendar keeps you on top of upcoming trending topics and events too, so you can plan content accordingly and reap the benefits.

Motivation can sometimes be a struggle when we're working for ourselves. Having dates, and a plan, to work to holds us accountable. Knowing what you have to get done and the deadlines you're working to, reduces stress. A calendar will improve your momentum and so traffic will start to build. As people will come looking for your new posts if you're consistent.

An editorial calendar allows you to bring all of your ideas together in one place. Everything you have pinned, made notes about and have written in your diary, can all be added to your editorial calendar, meaning you can work in a more focused and efficient manner. If you use the plugin as I do, then consider having a separate editorial calendar in Airtable or Asana where you can store your ideas.

There was a time when people thought multitasking was the way forward; the way to get stuff done. However, this is no longer the case. Studies of successful people have shown that focusing deep and narrow on one task at a time produces much more productivity. Having a calendar spells out to you where your focus should be.

If you're just publishing as and when you feel like it, you're relying totally on your memory to ensure that your posts are balanced. Having a visual aid makes it so much clearer to see where the different types of posts are and helps you spread the content out better.

Blogging can be hard. Having the key dates and your goals in front of you will help you keep things in perspective and allows you to plan content that will help you achieve your goals.

I think having an editorial calendar is such an important part of blogging and I literally couldn't blog without mine. It's a professional way to work, strategically planning posts, rather than simply chucking posts out there and hoping some of them will stick.

Let's get planning

The reason I love my editorial calendar is that it gives me a visual representation of my week and month. As said, I prefer the Editorial Calendar WordPress plugin, but even a spreadsheet or paper and pen will do the trick. Choose a method that fits with how you work. If you like paper planners stick with it, embrace it! This digital method suits me, as I can see gaps, drag and drop posts and get a really good handle on the upcoming days/weeks. I also use a few lists/boards in Airtable to help me keep track of where I'm up to with actually writing the posts. In addition, I also keep a running list of the post topics I want to write about in there too.

At this point, it's a good idea to think about how many times a week you want to post. Bear that in mind when you move onto the following steps.

The first thing I do when faced with a blank calendar is to slot in the regular posts, the posts I write each week. This might be a linky you run or that you join in with every week. Perhaps an update you always write at the same point each week or even each month.

To make this duplication much easier I use the **Copy to Draft** WordPress plugin. This allows me to set one post up with the information which will stay the same each week (maybe the linky badge or the structure of the post). Then, I just click the **Copy to Drafts** button a few times and lots of duplicate posts appear in the unscheduled drafts section of my editorial calendar. I simply drag these to the correct days on the calendar. Then, when it's time to write the post I can just add the specific information for each specific post. Now I have a great visual representation of my month and of the gaps I have to fill.

Next, you need to think about annual holidays or special dates. This partly depends on the type of content you create. You might choose to write content around the seasons, national days and the like. These dates are recurring, so you can just pop them in the calendar, way ahead of time.

Add in any commissioned posts from brands. I check the date they're due and pop them onto the calendar a few days before this deadline. That way if I move things around, I know I can pull the post earlier, but I would never push it later. Also, it means they're on the calendar so won't be forgotten about. The same goes for review posts. If I know we are going to an event or away on a reviewing break, I will put a post in the calendar for a few days after the visit, ready for our return. This keeps me on track and all of these posts top of mind.

I would then add in any personal content. Posts which would fall in this realm are updates on your kids, a birthday, an anniversary or maybe even your blog birthday.

Now it's time to jiggle! At this point, some of these posts aren't set in stone, you can move the posts around to fill any gaps you may have. It will also give you a consistent posting schedule (which remember Google loves!).

Point to note!

Occasionally, I might work with a brand who want to see a draft by a certain date. If this is the case I pop the draft in the calendar the day before the draft is due, then I can move it into place when I have approval. I might also put a blank (just titled) duplicate place holder post in the calendar on the date they want the post to go live. Then, I can drag the actual post over and delete the placeholder.

Do you have any extra posts to add?

I then fill out the rest of my calendar using my list of post ideas, then I'm good to go and start writing!

At the end of the content planning process, I used to have at least one post a day scheduled. Add into that sponsored opportunities that come up throughout the month and I would have two-four posts a day going out! Now, I'm further into my blogging and have come to my senses. I post between three-five times a week.

However often you post, it's so much easier to plan your content calendar in advance. Then you can hit the ground running, making the most of the time you have to create that great content!

ABY'S ACTION STEP

Plan out your next month of content using your chosen system. Slot in all the date-bound projects and work through the list to add in all the other content you need to produce during the next month. If you've already planned the next few months you can plan out your entire year. You might choose to theme each month to make content creation and promotion much easier and more cohesive.

How can you write all your content in the easiest way possible?

My favourite thing to do when creating content productively is to batch the tasks. In reality, an example would be when I will film multiple videos all in a block of time. This makes sense as you will be set up to film one, so you might as well keep rolling and do as many as you can. You can then batch edit them too. Batching is super productive as it eliminates the focus loss (and time loss too!) that happens when you switch between tasks.

Another thing I do is to batch edit pictures in Lightroom. This saves me hours, I can edit one image, then apply those edits to all the other selected pictures. Save them in a folder in Lightroom and export to my Mac into a folder of the same name, so I'm all good to go when it comes to writing the post.

Often, I will drop the pictures into a post and then write around them. It helps structure and recollection (especially for a day out or event post).
We're all under sizeable time pressure, so we need ALL the tips we can get to help us do more in less time. Writing posts can be a slow process depending on your style. *So how do you write faster and still maintain your quality?* Lots of us are juggling multiple commitments in our daily lives. Add in blogging and writing a single blog post can seem like an insurmountable task!

Firstly, remember how powerful your mind is. Have you heard of a self-fulfilling prophecy? If you're always telling yourself you're so slow at writing, 'oh, it'll take me forever to write that post,' then you know what? It will! Our subconscious mind is so powerful. So, change the way you talk to yourself and start being more positive; make it work for you. Instead, think, 'I'm so fast at writing my posts' and see what happens over time.

The process I mentioned earlier will come in useful to help you speed up your content creation. The post outline should include the key points you want to make in the three sections of your post; intro, body, and conclusion. Having this laid out will help you focus and will increase your writing speed.

Begin with the end firmly in mind. When people have read your post what do you want to them to think or feel; what's the action you want them to take? Then, when you know this you work backwards and reverse engineer your content to make sure you get your reader to this desired end point.

Always keep a topic list packed full of all your wonderful ideas. This list can be stored anywhere that works for you. Keeping a list of potential post topics means you never have to waste time procrastinating about what you will write and you can hit the ground running. I do this on a secret Pinterest board and also keep a running list in Airtable.

Planning your editorial calendar as I described earlier will speed up your content creation no end. You should also spend time brainstorming your content. Plan out your posts for the next six months or whatever timescale floats your boat. This takes away from any decision of what you'll write next when you have time to create content.

'Get it written not perfect'

This is so important! Lots of us can be quite self-critical and so when it comes to procrastinating we can be world record holders. **Just get it done!** Yes, you want it to be good, great even. Wonderful content that will enrich the lives of your readers. However, it never has a chance to enrich their lives if you never press *publish*. So, get it done, not perfect.

Writing is like a muscle, practice makes perfect. When you use a skill, it becomes stronger. If you write in a focused way, bearing these tips in mind, you will find it easier and easier to get into the habit, until it becomes second nature.

Utilising list posts can be a good way to speed up content creation. List are quicker and easier to write, as they enable you to break up the information you want to share into manageable chunks. These chunks are also far easier for your readers to digest. Not every post can be a list post, but they are used where appropriate.

One of my favourite things to do is to dictate posts onto my iPhone. I can dictate a post when I am getting ready for the day, when I am driving in the car, when I'm cooking; the possibilities are endless! Just open an email, address it to yourself, then click the microphone button and away you go.

'A task expands as if to fill the time given for its completion' - Parkinson's Law

If we give ourselves a day to write a post, chances are it will take a day. If we give ourselves two hours, you know what; we can do it in two hours, because we have a higher degree of motivation resulting from the deadline.

As solo workers, we don't have a boss to answer to or someone imposing deadlines onto us. This makes an accountability buddy such an amazing thing in terms of productivity for us solo workers. Finding someone at a similar level/stage to you and working together to keep each other accountable could be hugely beneficial for both of you.

Why content is still king?

"Content is king", I'm sure you've heard that before! When print content dominated and the internet was just a pipe dream; 'content is king' was the irrefutable truth. However, how even in today's world where online dominates print content, many of the world's top SEO and marketing experts still insist, "content is king."

"Content marketing is the only marketing left." - Seth Godin

Marketing has changed dramatically over the years. In recent years customers have been given more and more choice, so they are now more discerning than ever. Consequently, marketing activities that got results a few years ago probably won't do as well today.

Why is this the case? That even after decades, no matter the medium, content is still the crux of good marketing?

Content is the aspect of marketing which builds loyalty. Businesses aren't built on first-time visitors. Companies like the Wall Street Journal don't make the majority of their money from people purchasing their papers for the first time. They make the lion's share of their money from people who've read their content and then decided it was good enough to either purchase again or purchase a subscription. If the business had to get a new customer every time in order to get paid, they'd all have gone bust by now. Yet many online publications approach their business that way.

Instead of focusing on repeat visitors, they focus on optimising for search engines to attract more new customers. However, the really successful blogs like the Huffington Post, Gizmodo and LifeHacker still get most of their traffic from repeat visitors. Yes, they're great at the search engine stuff, but their businesses wouldn't be anywhere near as successful as they are today if they didn't have great content.

Google and other search engines are constantly working towards improving search results. They want people who search on their engines to find the best content possible in relation to what they're looking for. As search engines get smarter, it will become increasingly important to focus on quality content.

Google has proven this by continually downgrading the value of low-quality links and upgrading the importance of usage statistics and other metrics which measure the content of a website. If you build your blog on great quality content, while also having a good understanding of basic SEO, your site will be successful. However, if you focus solely on SEO and not on creating quality content, you might find yourself always trying to stay one step ahead of the search engines.

Will content always be king?

Great quality content allows you to build a relationship with your readers. This relationship then allows you to sell any number of things to your readers. Quality content will give you the opportunity to sell higher ticket products or programmes.

In the long run, only content that really helps people is going to succeed. Content that doesn't, is likely to get downgraded more and more as time passes.

Great content encourages readers to engage and share. Poor content will never get the same degree of engagement, if any at all. This engagement will really make a difference to the impact that your post has. So make sure your readers can share your posts easily and that you give your content a good airing on social media.

Consistently publishing quality content will transition your blog into an authority and creates many more opportunities for other sites to link to you, meaning a rise in backlinks. This will also have a significant impact on **SEO** and your blog's **SERP** (Search Engine Ranking Position), helping it rank organically for relevant search terms and keywords. The higher the ranking, the more potential traffic it can gain.

Your awesome original content will also help to drive traffic and lower your site's bounce rate. People will be more tempted to click on another post, if they can see your site is packed with fab information.

Focusing your efforts on your content, only publishing your very best stuff, will elevate your brand and give you an edge in a saturated market. The more awareness people have about your brand, the more chance you will have to convert this awareness into sign-ups to your email list and sales.

Content which adds value and solves a problem for your readers will always be favoured. Therefore, if your product can then be positioned in the same way i.e. helping them with their issue/problem, it will feel less 'salesy' and more congruent to your brand.

What is cornerstone content?

What do people need to know to make the best use of your blog and the information you provide? This is cornerstone content. Think of it as the foundation upon which your blog has been built.

This content will typically be super relevant and useful to your audience. They will be blog posts that provide your readers with huge amounts of value, inspiration, resources, and more. They will contain text, graphics, photos, charts, slide shares; whatever works for your post and for your audience. They will probably include content upgrades (opt-in freebies) too.

These posts aren't your standard 600-800 word blog posts, they will usually be around 1500 words up to even 5,000 words. They will be meaty and packed with epic value.

After you have done your best to make this content value-packed and relevant. It will also become content that people will want to link to and share. This will then help your SEO and again help to increase your backlinks. This sort of content can also add more weight to you being seen as an authority in that particular area.

How can you make the most of this cornerstone content and help your readers at the same time?

Well, you set up a cornerstone content page! This page can fall under different names; sneeze page, start here page; the list goes on. In essence, it's a page that you can direct people to, or that they can find easily on your menu bar. This page will walk your readers through your main posts and important areas of your blog, so you're doing the work for them. The more you can lay things out for people and make it easy for them, the better.

You could even have an opt-in box on this page, as people will be keen to sign up having read all the amazing content you've shared. This page will help you hold the reader's hand as they navigate around your site. It also means you are showing them what you want them to see first.

Obviously, they can click anywhere, but they would be silly not to follow your recommendations. They know you're going to direct them to the best content, so you will be saving them time.

In a lot of cases, this cornerstone content will be evergreen too. Evergreen content is content that's as valuable to the reader on the day they read it, as it was when the author wrote it, regardless of the time elapsed between the two.

There are four main forms of content to consider when creating any post; text, graphic, audio, and video. Each having its own benefits and drawbacks and each type appealing to different audiences.

Text-based content is the most common type of content on the internet by far. Just about every webpage you see is based on text content. The biggest benefit of text-based content is that it's very search engine friendly. Search engines can't understand videos or audios in the same way as they do text. Your SEO will be more effective, and you have more chance of ranking for your chosen keywords. It's also much easier to create text content. There's no need for expensive or complicated equipment, so it's accessible to everyone.

Graphic based content covers images, video, memes, screen shots, presentations and infographics. Graphics are often eye-catching and can be an effective way of transmitting bite-sized information in an engaging manner.

Audio content has grown in popularity with the rise of podcasts. Audio is more difficult to produce as the sound quality is crucial, so it does need some investment in equipment. Although it takes more effort to produce, it's a popular format as it makes content accessible for people to listen on the go. I know I'm a huge podcast fan and listen to them when doing house work, editing images or driving. I'm also co-host of a podcast called The Huddle, which you should totally check out by the way!

Video content is one of the most dynamic ways of sharing content and it works for most types of content. It's a great way to engage your audience, while helping to develop the know, like and trust factor. People love video and people frequently share videos on Facebook. A video has a much higher chance of going viral than say an audio podcast. Video content takes time to create and requires a good quality camera, although most smartphones are just fine. The editing can be a little technical, but it's nothing that can't be quickly learned from a YouTube tutorial.

Whatever form your cornerstone content takes, consider using a few different types of content in a single post. This will increase the post's appeal and it will become even more epic.

Start to think how you can lead your readers round your blog to give them the best possible experience. Don't forget the more time people spend on your site the better. Google's algorithm takes the time on site into account when deciding search engine rankings for a particular keyword search. They measure the time from when someone clicks through to your site from Google until they hit the back button and return to Google. So, you want them on your site for as long as possible.

ABY'S ACTION STEP

Think of who you write for. How do you best serve your audience? Identify their main needs and decide on the topics you could write about which fit these needs. Focus in on these areas and decide which specific sub topics you could create cornerstone content for. What do you want to be known for?

HOWEVER! The king can't rule the land alone!

Why content can't be all we focus on...

There will always be brilliant talented writers that don't succeed. Sad, but true. Fabulous, engaging content will not set you apart from the crowd on its own.

Nope, sadly it won't!

Promoting that awesome content is also super important. You can write as brilliantly as you like, or shoot the most engaging videos, but if no-one knows about them it doesn't matter how wonderful what you create is.

It's not as 'easy' as simply creating epic content. **EVERYONE** produces epic content. You need to **promote** it epically as well. This is where most people fall down.

Promotion is key. Oh, and conversion matters too…

Can you make the most of the visitors you get by **converting** them? Making a sale? Getting them to subscribe to your email list? If you can't, you will need to keep getting those new visitors again and again purely to keep your traffic numbers up. Instead, you need to '**funnel**' these visitors into something that will help them remember you (like signing up for your list or grabbing a freebie from you). This allows you to start building a relationship with them.

Sometimes the content that does well is just alright… Not brilliant or epic, just alright. Passable content. Maybe with a click bait headline added for good measure. Sometimes, average wins which proves that content is not always king *on its own*.

Amazing content will not always be the content that makes the most money either. Have you ever heard of the starving artist? Some of the sites with average content, but lots of traffic will be cashing in on revenue from ads.

Does this mean content is dead? No, it's definitely not. However, creating epic content alone is not going to guarantee your success. You need to also promote that content. Think outside the box and try to find 'your thing'. That thing that will help YOUR epic content stand out from everyone else's.

CHAPTER 6

The posts you need on your blog

As bloggers, we ALL want more traffic. We try to write posts that our readers will love. There are certain types of posts which have a longer-term appeal and can be a source of traffic for months and even years to come. This type of evergreen content can take many different forms.

If you can incorporate these posts, you will be positioning your blog well for lots of continued traffic. So it's well worth the time you will invest to create them.

1. Detailed review

This post is just as it sounds, a thorough review of a product or service. For this post, you really want to go all out on the detail and try to make it THE BEST review on that product/service. Make sure you capitalise on search traffic by including the word 'review' in the title of the post. This post is a prime candidate for affiliate links too.

If you use Amazon and your reader clicks through your link but doesn't buy that product, and they go on to buy something completely different, you will still get commission. As soon as a potential customer enters Amazon through one of your links they get a cookie on their browser which links them to you as an affiliate. As long as that cookie is active you will earn commissions on anything that customer purchases. This cookie can either be a 24-hour cookie or a ninety-day cookie.

The 24-hour one gives you the commission on anything they purchase for 24 hours. The ninety-day cookie gives you the chance to earn commissions on sales that are made up to ninety days after a user clicks on your affiliate link. However, there are things which need to happen in order for this cookie to be placed on the user's browser. If a reader goes through your affiliate link and buys something different within the 24-hour window you will get that commission. Plus, if they place the item you linked to in their basket within the 24 hour period, but don't check out, this then turns into a ninety-day window for commissions on that specific product only.

2. A complete guide

A complete guide is an awesome post to create as it is packed full of value and offers a step by step guide through a certain topic. These posts should be epic, contain different media types, but substantial in length (4-5k words) and might include videos in addition to photos. Remember it's a 'complete' guide.

3. Tech tutorial/walk through

This can be a walk through/tutorial of any tech you use. It could be an app on your phone, or a web-based programme or software. Even if you're a family blogger and don't blog about tech, you might use a money management app on your phone for household finances, or an app that has put you in touch with other local parents. This would be a great opportunity to share the detail of that programme with your readers. The format could be a picture and text walk through or even a screen share video.

4. Tools and resource guide

This post can be written for any niche and you could even have multiple versions for different topics within your niche. For me, it would be a blogging tool/resources guide. However, I could also have a photography equipment guide or one for live streaming. The possibilities are endless. As with the *detailed review* post, this post is a great candidate for affiliate links.

5. Before and after

This post will draw in the traffic if you pick a great topic. A topic where you can demonstrate a transformation is what we're looking for here. Think before and after weight loss, or before and after you started to use a particular system or software. You need to visually demonstrate the before and after, so screenshots and photographs should be included.

6. Disprove a myth

What's the biggest myth in your industry? Clean eating is boring. Bloggers need massive traffic to earn an income. Vegetarian food is bland. You get the picture. Pick your 'myth' and then create your post to disprove it.

7. Your story

This is a must-have for any blog. Remember, your readers have to connect with you, in order to want to come back time and time again. By sharing your story, you're giving them so much more information to find resonance with. Sharing your story can be really powerful and this is why it's a must-have post.

8. Case study

A case study is a detailed deep dive into a specific topic. The focus could be on something you have done or a friend or client. Again, weight loss could make a good case study. It could also be something like 'How to pass your driving test in 5 days'. This post should be detailed and would include screenshots, timescales and be full of facts and figures.

9. Controversial post

This post might not be for the faint hearted, but you know the saying, 'faint heart never won fair maiden'! Sometimes you have to take a stand and polarise people. Stop being 'beige' and stand up for what you believe in. No doubt you will have people who disagree with you,

BUT you'll find 'your' people and they will love you for sharing your views so openly with the world.

10. Comparison post

This is similar to a review post, but here you're comparing two similar systems, items, programmes or products. You will have detailed information on both and you will present the pros and cons in your post.

11. List post

This is one post type that I'm quite confident you will have already. List posts are a staple for most blogs. They break up information, so it's easy to consume and they're also super easy to create too.

12. Cheat sheet/checklist

Checklists and cheat sheets are the perfect freebies to add to any post to help build your email list. The topics could be *almost* anything. 'Best beauty buy' checklist, '10 steps to building your Twitter followers,' literally anything can be made into a cheat sheet or checklist.

13. Infographic

Infographics are a great thing to create for your posts. You can also find infographics others have created to include in posts. To find infographics, search infographic + KEYWORD and then use the embed code to pop it in your post. All you have to do is to write a few paragraphs and you're good to go! Infographics containing statistics are a great option and are always well received.

14. Definition post

The definition post is a really useful post to have on your blog, especially for newbies. A terms glossary for your niche or interest area is a great resource which people will keep referring to. You could also include a print out of this list as an opt-in freebie to build your list too!

15. FAQ post

A 'frequently asked questions' post can be a really useful addition to your audience, but it can also help you too. It can answer the questions you get asked a lot and therefore reduce people's need to ask you again. You can also direct people to the post instead of rewriting the information multiple times. For me, the questions I get asked all the time are things like, which camera do I use? How do I prioritise? Which systems do I use to get stuff done? How do I automate? How do you hire a VA?

16. Expert advice

The expert advice post can be a fun one to create. Find three experts in your niche and ask them a question. For entrepreneurs, it could be 'the best piece of advice they have ever received.' For vegetarians 'how they got started and their biggest challenge.' People love learning about other's lives and so these types of posts are usually popular posts. The chosen experts will also usually share the post with their audience, which will lead to more traffic.

17. Beginner's guide

The beginner's guide is similar the *complete guide*, but for this one, you are focused on people at the start of their journey only. For me, it could be '7 days to start a blog', or 'the beginner's guide to WordPress'. Everyone starts somewhere in any niche, and new people start every day, which means you should have a constant supply of traffic to this post.

ABY'S ACTION STEP

For each of these post types, I want you to brainstorm ideas for a post you could write for each post type.

CHAPTER 7

Our first press trips

I began to work harder and harder, partly to keep up with the demands asked of me and partly because that's my nature. I'm driven. I like to work hard and become involved in projects. The more I did, the bigger the rewards were that came back to me.

The opportunities we were offered became more exciting and through my blog (in January 2015) we went on our first holiday in five years. It was also Ava's first ever holiday. Bluestone Wales had invited us and we were so happy to get the chance to go away as a family. The only bump in the road was my husband leaving Ava's suitcase at home! However, the silver lining in that particular cloud was a shopping trip to the local Next and almost a completely new wardrobe! Our finances weren't great and so this opportunity provided us with the family holiday, which we wouldn't have been able to afford otherwise. It felt like another world.

We shared the experience with a couple of blogging friends who were there with their families, which was so lovely. While we were enjoying our holiday, I received a very exciting email. I was invited on a press trip to Rome hosted by Bridgestone Tyres. The trip would take place in April and it would be just myself, with some other bloggers/journalists. I couldn't wait to accept but I was worried about leaving my husband and Ava. However, as always my super supportive husband encouraged me to go for it, so I did.

Rome was amazing. In addition to the press parts of the trip, they had organised so many amazing dinners and even a trip to a vineyard. We enjoyed a guided-tour round Rome, taking in the Colosseum and various other architectural highlights. It was totally mind-blowing. During 2015 we also went on two other family review trips, and I remained constantly amazed each time an opportunity came my way.

While I was in Rome, I received the news that I had made the shortlist in the 'family' category at the annual Brilliance in Blogging awards. To say I was happy was an understatement! At the start of my blogging journey I never imagined anyone would even read my blog. Yet here I was twenty months later, genuinely thrilled that people had taken the time to vote for me and got me to the shortlist.

So far, I've been a finalist three times (2015, 2016, 2017) in different categories and although I'm always the bridesmaid, it's a real thrill to make it each year.

The first sixteen months recap

When I think back to all the wonderful things blogging has done for me I actually feel tearful. Not in a negative way, I promise you they are happy tears! Blogging has been so powerful and exceptionally influential in my life. Taking stock of that can sometimes feel overwhelming. So much happened during my first sixteen months that I will always be exceptionally grateful for. I received so much support and the changes in my blog were incredible.

In that first year and a half, blogging went from a much-loved hobby — something I did a few times a week — to my job. To something that is such a part of me, I couldn't bear to stop. If you cut me in half I would have the word blogger running through me like a stick of rock.

My blog climbed from being ranked 1300+ to 68 in the Tots100 charts, which is a league for UK for parenting lifestyle bloggers including 10-15k blogs. My Twitter following soared from 300 to almost 7k. The cobbled together header changed into a beautiful custom design. In other words, it was entirely different after a mere sixteen months. This isn't me bragging, that's not my style, it's just to show that with hard work, anyone with the passion, can let blogging change their life.

In August 2015, my blog turned two. I remember feeling very emotional about what my blog meant to me when I sat down to write an anniversary post. It had given my family so much in only 24 months. **I felt it had given me myself back.**

Towards the end of 2015, I felt the blog needed a change. I wanted something less 'cute' and so in the absence of an available designer, I set to revamping my blog myself. I bought a new theme and later that day, the new You Baby Me Mummy was born — I work quickly!) I added a new tagline, which would weed out the Dirty Dancing fans ('nobody puts baby in the corner' as my daughter's blog nickname was baby). A sleeker look, yet still with personality and colour.

Even two years into my blogging journey, I would often feel overwhelmed and emotional when I reflected on what blogging had done for me. The most important thing that blogging has given me since I started is the most amazing friends.

Before I started, I would never have believed that you can be friends with people that you have never met or only briefly in some cases. I now know better. I have such genuine wonderful friendships with so many incredible women, who I have found through writing my blog.

Some of these ladies have become my very my best friends and I remain to this day so very grateful for each and every one of them. We laugh, love, support, care, inspire and motivate each other. I feel so lucky that I found this world of blogging and to have found these bright, amazing women. These are women that, in some cases, I speak to every day via social media, phone or text message. They are women that have come to mean so much to me and whom I wouldn't have found without my blog.

Ready to take your first step? Well, you need to find your voice honey.

"I write only because there is a voice within me that will not be still." -Sylvia Plath

What's your blogging voice?

Have you ever read a post and felt as if the author was talking directly to you? You felt like you were friends or that at the very least that you should be! You can tell they're passionate, self-expressed and they speak with confidence. People are moved by those who speak with their real voice. Yet, what most people don't realise is that almost everyone who has found their voice has had to put in a lot of work to find that voice. It doesn't usually come naturally.

When you read something that has been written from personal experience, you get a sense of the person who wrote it. If they write well their personality will jump off the page. Their writing could make you feel as if you know them personally, when all you have actually done is read their words. They have the skill to make you *'feel'*; they can engage you and take you on a journey with their words.

'Your voice' isn't *one thing. I*t's everything about how you communicate. Your writing style, your tone and your choice of words. If you have a strong voice, it may well polarise people. Not everyone will like you and you know what? That's just fine. In order to find our true fans, we will come across people who just do not find a resonance with our message and prefer to go elsewhere. Let them go and just know that you're one step closer to finding people who will LOVE your voice.

There's no doubt that you can develop your voice to make it stronger and more representative of you. However, it will not happen overnight.

There are lots of ways to approach finding your voice, so let's get started.

Start with what you're passionate about

If you love internet marketing, get into the internet marketing field. If you love crocheting, get into the crocheting field. Ask yourself: What's a topic that you could talk about for hours and hours on end?

What's a topic that you'd talk about and obsess about even if you weren't getting paid? What's something that really lights you up in life and gets you excited? While not every passion can be turned into a career, you'd be surprised at how many people do manage to turn their passions into money, even in very obscure fields. Start with what you're really passionate about. It'll come through in your voice.

I recently met a lovely lady who had successfully monetised her American farm, specifically focusing on the llamas she owns. Now if that's not niche, I don't know what is!

Be as self-expressed as possible

Now, this can be a challenge, but try to write without censorship. Don't worry too much about the grammatical or political correctness. In reality if you're speaking with your *real* voice, you're probably going to turn some people off.

However, you'll also really attract the kinds of people you should be attracting. You won't successfully grow your platform by trying to please everyone. When you're writing content, try to write as if you're speaking one-to-one with a friend of yours. Write naturally, in a casual yet self-expressed and passionate manner. You will find your content is much more relatable to your audience if you do.

Care about the impact you want to make

I'm sure you can tell the difference between someone who's written something and who really cares about your success, versus someone who's just writing the content to write the content? Most likely, you can tell that the former has a completely different feel. Naturally, it's the people who genuinely want to help us that we feel drawn to. When you're writing content ask yourself, who are you trying to help with this content? How would you like their life to change as a result of you writing this content for them? If you really want to help people, they can sense that. It comes through in your writing and creates loyalty.

Be consistent

While you don't have to have the same tone in all your posts (i.e. being funny or sarcastic) you do need to have the same voice. When your readers read a post they ideally should recognise your voice shining through.

I always write the way I speak, so it's easy for me to maintain consistency across all my posts. Also, through live video and when I meet people in person. Chopping and changing would be off-putting for my readers and wouldn't give them a sense of knowing the *real* me.
Make sure you're staying true to your voice. Whether you're writing a post, speaking on stage, chatting on a call, whatever! There needs to be a consistency to your voice, in order to build the know, like and trust factor and in turn help to build your credibility.

Write like you speak

From a young age, we are taught to write in a formal way. We write letters, we pass exams, fill out forms, write essays and none of these forms of writing require us to show our personality. All of them demand formality and correctness.

They don't help us to develop our skills for emotive writing that connects with our readers. Just imagine you're talking to a friend when you write and it will help you lose the formality.

Read (and write!) lots to stay inspired to share your voice.

"The best way to develop your writer's voice is to read a lot. And write a lot. There's really no other way to do it." - Stephen King

As you're reading, think about what you like about the author's writing style. Which aspects could you take into your own style?

I'm constantly inspired by other content creators and think this is one of the best ways to find YOUR voice. The more you write, the more time you will have to find and hone your voice. Practice makes perfect!

Copying, but not copying

"Nobody is born with a style or a voice. We don't come out of the womb knowing who we are. In the beginning, we learn by pretending to be our heroes. We learn by copying." - Austin Kleon

Humans learn by modelling. So, why don't we use modelling to help us develop our writing voice? I don't mean copying everything someone else does.
Rather being inspired and taking inspiration from an aspect that we can do our way. The best way to work through this is to pick a writer you admire and who you resonate with. Then ask yourself these questions;

- Why do you love their writing style?
- What is it about their hooks that compel you to read on?
- Why is their tone different?
- Do they have words they use frequently?
- Do they share their life stories?
- Do they inspire you to take action?

Let the answers to these questions feed into your own voice. Have the confidence to do things your way.

ABY'S ACTION STEP

Think about the writers you love. Why do you love them? What makes them special? How do they tell stories? Use this to inform your own writing development.

Tell a story

As bloggers we know we should give value. Often we focus so much on giving the content in a clear way that we forget to share ourselves too. Your readers want to know your opinion on something. They don't just want the facts. They want your version, your opinion, and your stories.

Your stories are unique to you, so sharing them shows your audience the real you and also gives them those all-important chances to resonate with your message.

Make sure you have a point

Have you ever read a post got to the end and wondered if you missed the point? You skim down it again, but, nope, you didn't miss anything. There wasn't really a point. You don't want to do that to your readers. You don't want them to feel like they wasted the time they spent on your site. Your posts must have a point and your voice should help you communicate this point to your readers.

As you get more confident in your writing ability, you will start to show more of your personality in your posts. Don't be in a hurry to rush or force anything. Even years into my blogging journey, I still find myself adding more and more of myself to the content I write.

Reading your posts aloud is a wonderful way to hear how they sound first hand. Does it sound forced or natural? You want your words to sound like an easy conversation. If blogging starts to feel like a chore it will show in your writing. So, make sure you always love what you do. This will project from your posts and draw people in. Be confident that your voice is worth hearing. You have as much right to tell your story as anyone else, so share your story and share part of you too.

Showing your readers your personality means they will be able to identify with you so much more. Be honest, be truthful and most of all be you.

As I said, a strong blogging voice can sometimes be polarising, but voicing your opinions is important. To be seen as a leader, then you will need to add a strong dose of personality to what you do online.

Stop worrying whether people might not like you. Let your personal quirkiness shine through. Feel free to be different, eccentric, or even a bit weird. That's how you connect, and engage, and grow your blog following.

Do you think you've found your true writing 'voice'?

ABY'S ACTION STEP

I want you to start keeping track of the idiosyncrasies in the language you use. What do you always say to friends? Do you have common words you use? Phrasing? How do you really speak? I want you to take these and write them down. This stuff is gold dust and it's 'you'. Then you can use this book to help you write your content in a way that reflects you more fully.

CHAPTER 8

Focus on your why and the who.

There's another factor that often gets over looked. People start their blog, they put their time and energy into it. Then sometimes they're left wondering why they don't get the return they hoped for in the form of traffic and community. The answer would usually be because they've not kept aligned with their '*why*'.

In terms of careers and hobbies blogging is quite new. It's only been around for just over twenty years. This means there are lots of people who still don't 'get' blogging or understand what it is that us bloggers *actually* do. My mother included! I swear she thinks I just post pictures on Facebook all day.

Although this can be frustrating at times, the fact that blogging isn't as established as more 'traditional' careers means that to some degree we can use it to create whatever we want in our lives. It gives us more flexibility and scope to make things happen. Which can be extremely exciting.

However, in order to use it to its full potential, we need to really understand our 'why'. We need to ask ourselves *why* we blog and have real clarity in our answer. Otherwise, we will never be truly focused enough to reach our full potential.

What's your motivation? What are your objectives for blogging? Why did you start in the first place? What keeps you going when things get rough? What are your underlying passions and aims of your blog? These are all really useful questions that if you spend time and answer honestly, they will get you closer to finding your *why*.

Then, when you have brainstormed this and have total clarity, you need to work out who your ideal reader is. Why? Because you're going to want to write to them specifically.

'If you try to attract everyone, you will attract no-one'

This is the part that so many people are resistant to at the start. When you suggest this as a course of action, they push back and often want to avoid it altogether. You see, we ALL want to be liked by everyone.

So, at the start of our online careers we tend to go middle of the road with everything we do. Middle of the road doesn't often make people dislike you, BUT it doesn't often make people love you either. You need to have confidence to stand in your own truth and share who you are through your content. Remember, if some people don't like it, that's totally fine, they are just making room for those who will love you.

'If people don't like you, don't worry they're just not your people'

How to figure out who your ideal reader is?

I too resisted this part for so long. I didn't want to think about just one reader. If I'm honest I thought it was a bit weird, making up a story about an imaginary person. I mean who has time for that....! But have you ever read something and felt as if the author was talking directly to you? As if they're taking the thoughts and feelings right from your head. You felt so connected to what they were saying and you really resonated with them.

This level of connection is achieved by the writer knowing exactly who their ideal reader was. They didn't make that awesome connection by hedging their bets and writing for a whole group of people. Nope, they went specific. They knew their ideal reader inside and out and they wrote their content directly to that one person.

Your ideal reader avatar is simply a fictitious character that you have created to represent your audience. In reality, no-one's message is a good fit for every single reader. That's just not realistic. Your message might resonate with women more than men, or with the older generation more than the younger generation. It's such a mistake to think we can serve all the people in the same way. It's simply not possible. The more detailed and specific you can get when creating your ideal customer avatar, the more chance you have of creating a message that truly resonates with the people you're trying to reach.

What should your ideal customer avatar include?

The key to being able to create a really strong message is to have a **very** detailed customer avatar. This avatar should include every detail you can think of about your ideal reader. It will include demographic and psychographic information down to things like their favourite TV shows and the nail colour they like to wear. It really does pay to go deep.

After you've created your avatar you will know exactly who you're trying to attract. What motivates them? What's important to them? How can you best reach them? You might find your ideal avatar sounds a lot like you. Potentially at an earlier stage of their lives or journey than you. That's totally fine. Often we gravitate to people that are similar to ourselves.

Shall I show you mine?

Meet Daisy. Daisy is in her early 30s she lives in Cornwall with her husband Mike and her two young kids Lily who's four and Evie who's two. Daisy has had jobs before in her life that she has enjoyed, even loved, but she has always wanted more. Her family is the most important thing to her and she started her blog by chance just as a creative outlet whilst at home with her young children. Daisy feels she has potential, which she's not sure how to fully utilise and this frustrates her. She wants to make her blog a success, but she worries about finding the balance with her family life. Not wanting to miss out on anything involving her girls.

Her husband earns good money and the family is financially secure, but Daisy still wants to turn her blog into a business and make it a success. She has a degree in Art Therapy and would love to continue to develop her skills, using them in her blog and future business. She is an organised person, but gets frustrated that she often doesn't know where to start or which direction to go in with her blog. She does have the faith though, that her blog will give her and her family a better life.

She is obsessed with Friends and loves leopard print, much to her husband's amusement. She loves getting outdoors (listening to marketing/business podcasts while walking her dogs) and also loves her home comforts. A bath, magazine and an hour of peace is her idea of perfection.

This is a snapshot of Daisy, my ideal reader. Can you see how this makes it easy for me to write my messages and content directly to Daisy? This means my message will resonate with those people who are like Daisy to greater or lesser extent. My message may not resonate as much with Bob, a 55-year-old 'type A' man who wants to use his online platform to sell in a much harder way than Daisy, but you know what? That's OK. Not every blogger should or even can appeal to every possible reader. Just like not every brand's message will appeal to every consumer. You can't make everyone happy, you're not Nutella!

Begin to think about your 'ideal' reader, which magazines do they read? Where do they hang out online? Which TV shows do they enjoy? What car do they drive? The reason? You can never have too much detail about your ideal reader.

ABY'S ACTION STEP

Create your ideal reader avatar. Right down to their favourite TV show and all the details about their family and their lives. You literally can't go deep enough on this. Have some fun. Who would be the perfect person to read your content or buy your products and services?

Understanding your ideal reader so you can serve them better

We are all bombarded with content and sales messages every single day. You only have to go on Facebook for more than twenty seconds and you'll probably see multiple adverts flashing up on your screen. In order for your message to stand out, it must hit home. It will only hit home if it is specific. Part of a general message may appeal to more people, but they will never feel as if you're talking to them directly.

When you've brainstormed your ideal reader you will know everything about them. You will, therefore, know what language to use, how to market to them, what their pain points are. You will know their struggles, which products they will love and so much more.

What are their pain points?

Talking about pain points might sound a little weird. Now, you know EXACTLY who you're talking to, you need to get a full understanding of what your ideal reader is struggling with. What do they need to understand right now? Where are they getting stuck? What are their pain points?

Most businesses sell products and writers create content to solve a problem their customers/readers have. Part of creating your ideal reader avatar is digging deep enough to understand their emotions, their frustrations, and their pain points.

When investigating their pain points and core desires it's always useful to ask 'so that' at the end of each point you come up with. Sometimes the answer people might give is the surface desire and not their real core desire. Asking the question 'so that' helps you dig deeper into each aspect and really establish the specific pain point your content should be addressing.

For example, if someone said their desire was to lose weight, you would ask 'so that?' *So that* they could become more confident – '*so that?*' They can enjoy their family time more. In this case, the core desire of the weight loss is better, more enjoyable family time. The message might be constructed differently to that for someone who, for example, wanted to lose weight '*so that*' they looked better in their bikini.

Defining your ideal reader avatar will make sure you avoid marketing miscommunications, which could lead to no-one feeling connected enough to read your post or buy your products.

Staying focused on your ideal avatar allows you to share your content with them in a way which will appeal to them, while still representing the values of your brand.

You will have all of this insight because you did the research and you know who you are talking to, what they want, what they NEED and you will know how you can help them.

How do you know what their 'pain points' are?

If you already have an audience, maybe an email list, Facebook page or group, the easiest way is to simply ask them what their biggest struggle is. Polls always work well for this, people love to give their opinion, especially when it's easy for them to take part.

If you're just starting out and haven't got an audience yet, then you can use the Google search bar to delve deeper. Put in the keyword you are interested in, then look at the results which show the questions people want answers to.

You could also use answerthepublic.com which is a great resource. However, don't forget that you can always use other people's Facebook groups to research pain points. This will give you a better idea of pain points of people who are similar to your ideal reader than a whole heap of

Google results. The questions people are asking time and time again are current their pain points. Just make sure those asking the questions are your ideal readers, so don't just stalk any group

ABY'S ACTION STEP

1. *Think about why you want to blog? Or if you have a blog, why do you do it?*
2. *What is your message? If someone came to your blog would they know what your content is all about?*
3. *If you were writing your blog obituary in five-ten years' time what would you want it to say?*
4. *What are the top three pain points of your audience?*

It takes a village to grow a blog

Have you heard the saying, '*it takes a village to raise a child*'? Well, I think the same theory applies to our blogs.

Countless amazing aspects of my own blogging journey can attribute to the fact that I am working with others. As bloggers, our working time can be quite solitary. There are no days in the office and lunches with friends. There's no chatting with colleagues over a cup of tea (more's the pity!).

Instead, we trade this social side of our working lives, for the flexibility to work from home, be our own bosses and have a fluid schedule. One that enables us to drop the kids off at school and be able to collect them at the end of the day too. These wonderful benefits of our working lives can mean we're often burning the midnight oil alone.

As bloggers, we asked the universe to make our dreams come true. To enable us to create a life where our passion is also our job. However, it can feel like the universe gave with one hand, while taking the social aspects of our working life with the other.

However, it doesn't have to be like that. Blogging can be collaborative in so many ways. Not only that, but collaborations could be one of the best things you can do for your blog.

I recently answered a question in an interview, which asked what had been my favourite collaboration so far? I thought about all the brands I had worked with, and there were some wonderful brands and projects. However, I thought of the times I had collaborated with other bloggers and realised these were my favourite projects without doubt.

There's something hugely energising and powerful in the power of *we*. From the first challenge I ran; Project Productivity to present day in my membership programme, the Revolution Inner Circle, I watch awesome people support each other every single day.
They become each other's cheer-leaders; which never ceases to amaze me. People feel more powerful and positive with respect to their own life because they are part of something; part of a team all striving for a common goal.

Over the years I've been part of many fabulous team efforts. As part of the incredible Team Honk, dancing for six hours non-stop in Wembley Stadium to raise money for Comic Relief. Together with my wonderful friend Amy, I spearheaded the Save Syrian Children campaign, which mobilised a group of bloggers and together we raised thousands for Save The Children/Syrian Refugees campaign.

I have seen bloggers unite and raise money for all sorts of charities, do impactful work, head campaigns and make a real difference to the world in which we live. It's pretty inspiring stuff. I've also seen bloggers rally round to help each other when one of us is in crisis. Whether that help is organising funds for someone, or simply supporting them on social media. We have each other's backs. It's as simple as that.

Besides the huge good that can be done externally, the power of we can also be felt more personally. You become more motivated and driven when you're part of a 'we'. I have written joint blogs, ran collaborative links and even have a fabulous Instagram community with Amy (#LittleFierceOnes).

Our hashtag, was an idea that came to us over dinner, we created it and it's now a huge hashtag community. I attribute that to the power of we. These things, I know I wouldn't have accomplished on my own, but the power of *we* made me stronger and ultimately made me more successful.

The very best kind of friendships

When I was growing up I had a few close friends. They may have changed as I got older, but they were always a small group. I spent most of my youth riding horses and fell into a serious relationship at an early age. So, while I have had my share of nights out, most of them have been as part of a couple. I was never part of a large 'girl gang'. I didn't do the hanging around town thing that most kids do with their friends or the girls holidays as you get older. I was always at the stables or away competing my horse.

When I got back into horses after moving to the south of England, my circle of friends expanded quite dramatically. I started to work as an event organiser within the equine industry and consequently ending up knowing everyone! Some friends were closer than others, but when I fell pregnant, developed PND and eventually quit my job. I found that none of those 'friends' stuck around. I'll tell you something, going from knowing so many people with my phone ringing off the hook, to knowing no-one is quite a shock to the system. A few 'old' friends remained, but there was a void in my life. A void that, if I'm truly honest, was never really full in the first place.

When I was younger I had some friends that I thought were good friends. However, they were hard work and it always felt as if I was the one making all the effort and all of the allowances, which was exhausting. I started to think that this was normal. That maybe I *should* be the one that makes all the effort. I now know friendship should be a joyful experience, not an exhausting one. I have a couple of fabulous 'mummy' friends, who I met since having Ava, these gorgeous stalwart friends that aren't going anywhere.

I used to wonder what I'd done wrong. Why didn't I have this 'gang' that everyone else seemed to have? I often felt on the outskirts of these friendship circles, not quite 'good' enough to really be valued and involved. Why didn't I have friends you could message at any time of the day or night; the ones that would have your back?

That is until I started my blog, something I didn't see coming in the slightest when I typed that first post. Now I feel I have the *girl gang* I missed out on when I was younger. I have people who have my back. People who inspire me and people who I love being around. We message frequently, in some cases constantly (Katy, Ceri, Amy, and Jade!) and even those who I know a little less well still have a big impact on my life because we share so much. There's a common understanding. The amazing thing about blogging is that it helps you find people who are so similar to you and any physical distance between you doesn't matter.

Working on the internet and being friends with people who do exactly the same, is the factor which makes these relationships so special. As a whole, the blogging community is such a supportive place, but I have such a close relationship with four bloggers and our communication is pretty constant. Not something I had experienced before in friendships.

When I am burning the midnight oil writing posts, I know they will be doing the same. It seems a little odd but knowing that makes me feel less alone. I know one little message is all it will take to reach one of them and we often chat in the early hours of the morning. All of us in the same boat. If I need to chat about anything, work related or personal. I know they will be there as my sounding board and that they will give me the best advice I could get.

My new girl gang is made up of mainly lifestyle and parenting bloggers (or at least that is where they started!). I would love to introduce four of these wonderful women to you. Each one of them is incredible and it doesn't feel right not to formally introduce them. I haven't mentioned all the wonderful friends I've met through blogging as that would be a book by itself, but these women impact me every day and so they needed to be in a book about how my life changed. As they helped to change it.

Amy from AmyTreasure.com blogs about her amazing foodie creations. She's the most talented writer and photographer. Seriously, this lady could make a bin bag looks like a Chanel LBD! One of the very best friends anyone could have, FACT!

Next up, is Katy from WhatKatySaid.com who is my blogging rock. She's so generous with her time to everyone. Writing a fabulous family lifestyle blog, she's an organisational dream and makes running a successful blog and family look like a breeze. I'm so lucky to have her in my life.

Ceri… Well, what can I say about Ceri (cerigillett.com)? Well, I could tell you about the time she accosted Pat Flynn (yes THE Pat Flynn) in a bar in London and brought him over to me like I'd won him in a raffle. Maybe more on that later…. Ceri is a business powerhouse. She matches me in her work obsessiveness and we share a worryingly large amount of love for Gifs, which we frequently use as our primary means of communication. Ceri is my partner in crime for so many ventures (not least The Huddle podcast) and I can't think of anyone better to go through my crazy entrepreneurial journey with than her.

Lastly, but by no means least, Jade. I first met Jade when she was a follower of my blog and a great member of my free Facebook group. I knew she was special. The most helpful and kind person I think I've ever met. I knew I had to get her to work for me. She's a blogger in her own right over at <u>mummieswaiting.com</u>, but I'm so happy that she accepted my proposal to work as my Virtual Assistant. She has since become a wonderful friend too, which is such a huge bonus.

I genuinely never thought that friendships would turn out to be the best thing about blogging when I started, but I'm so glad they are.

Why are these friendships so special?

My blogger friends

They are strong, inspirational people. Blogging is demanding, especially when you're either working or have children to look after as well. To succeed you need to put in lots of work and effort and the people who are willing to do this have certain characteristics. This means

I'm surrounded by strong, inspirational people, with drive and determination.

These friends will never say, "Oh you got that for free!" They understand the relentless picture taking and need to 'just Instagram this picture'. Bloggers are the only community where you can all sit round a table, all be on your phones and for no-one to consider it rude!

They're so supportive. I've never been in a community that's as supportive as the blogging one. If you have an issue you can bet your bottom dollar that one of your blogger friends will help you out.

Bloggers are such a diverse and eclectic mix of people. Even within our niche, I know lawyers, stay at home parents, teachers, business owners, professional bloggers, to name a few. This makes for a great mix of people and ideas meaning ours a truly exciting niche.

They are omnipresent! Not many friends would respond to a message or tweet at midnight, but you can be assured that whatever time you are blogging, someone else will be too. Bloggers are never far from their phones or tablets; they always feel as if they're with you. I'm definitely in more regular contact with my blogging friends than with friends who don't blog. This regular contact results in your relationship strengthening.

Totally unexpected and pretty awesome

In September 2016, Ava and I were at a wonderful event. We were staying at a gorgeous hotel with lots of other bloggers in Gloucestershire. Late one night, I got a congratulations message and a garbled voicemail from a blogging friend to tell me to check out a link and that I'd made it into the final of the MAD (Mum and Dad) blog awards, in the Outstanding Contribution category. I was totally gob-smacked. For people to feel as if I, three years into my journey, deserved to stand alongside nine other amazing bloggers was wonderful. I stood beside people blogging through their partner's illness, people who were prolific fundraisers; real heroes.

That night I don't think anyone was thinking about winning, but rather, we stood there together proud of what bloggers can do. Especially when we work together. I felt so proud to also be sharing the stage alongside one of my best friends (and fellow blogger) Amy. *It was an incredible moment and such a gift.*

So, if you have an idea, a burning desire to do something, to change your blog, to change the lives of others, hell to change the world! Go out there and find your people. Find the people who share the same desires as you, find your '*we*' and nothing will be impossible.

Have I convinced you? OK then.

Let's build your community!

Let's build a community

Building a community around your blog is so important for its future success. Personally, I credit community with a great deal of the success I've experienced with my blog. Developing a thriving, supportive community really made a difference to the speed at which my blog grew.

'Community is built on values.'

Community is not just a group of people being in the same place at same time. Community is not what you're doing, but *why* you're doing it.

'People come for the content but stay for the community.'

This is so true, especially when we're talking about blogging. I experience this in my main Facebook group, The Mamapreneur Revolution, but especially in my membership the Revolution Inner Circle. There's no doubt that there is awesome content associated with both of my groups, but the community aspect is what makes people want to stay. If your blog can develop this community; yes people will come initially for your epic, useful content, but they will stay for the community that you've created.

So, what makes an awesome community? During the research for his book 'Expert Secrets,' Russell Brunson studied many mass movements, such as Nazi Germany and Christianity, to name a couple. He found that they all have three things in common. Now, you might be thinking, 'hang on Aby, I'm writing a blog not going to war' and you're right of course, but you can still use these theories to build a community around your blog. You might not be creating a mass movement but implementing a fraction of these ideas will make a difference to how easily you can build the community you desire.

The three features present in all mass movements

• **Charismatic leader/attractive character**
They all had a strong, charismatic leader. Someone who had an attractive, magnetic personality.

• **Future-based cause**
The cause they were all striving for was a future goal, that wasn't directly related to one person's personal gain. It was a perceived collective good. For me, this future

based cause for the mums I help is the freedom that they all want and that they gain from working from home.

- **Offer their audience a vehicle of change**

Each of these mass movements provided their followers with a vehicle of change. A path showing them how they would get from where they were at the start to this 'ideal' future position. The mass movements didn't just focus on the future-based cause, but HOW the followers would get there.

Remember, we can distil parts of these theories to use in our blogs/communities. Think of the principles and keep them in mind when you start to grow your own community.

But, why is community important, Aby?

Having a strong community will ensure you have a core band of loyal readers who will come back regularly to your site. This means that you don't have to attract a whole new audience each month. Kevin Kelly became known for his essay, 1,000 True Fans, of which the premise is:

'To make a living as a craftsperson, photographer, musician, designer, author, animator, app maker, entrepreneur, or inventor you need only a thousand of true fans.'

You might be thinking what constitutes a 'true fan,' Kelly goes on to explain;

'A true fan is defined as a fan that will buy anything you produce. These diehard fans will drive 200 miles to see you sing; they will buy the hardback and paperback and audible versions of your book; they will purchase your next figurine sight unseen; they will pay for the "best-of" DVD version of your free YouTube channel; they will come to your chef's table once a month. If you have roughly a thousand of true fans like this (also known as super fans), you can make a living — if you are content to make a living but not a fortune.'

As your relationship with your audience develops they will turn into an army of advocates for your brand. They will share your content, as they feel invested in the community and want to spread its message. The fact that other people are promoting your content for you, adds to the social proof. It makes your content more desirable, than if you shared it yourself.

'Social proof is a psychological phenomenon where people assume the actions of others reflect correct behaviour for a given situation. This effect is prominent in ambiguous social situations where people are unable to determine the appropriate mode of behaviour, and is driven by the assumption that surrounding people possess more knowledge about the situation.' Wikipedia

For me personally, community has been important for my own soul too. I always say that the people have been the best thing about blogging without a doubt. Having an awesome community around your blog is amazing for your own good, for your sanity, and for your happiness.

There's nothing worse than speaking to crickets. If you share something on social media and nothing happens but tumbleweed, then brands won't see you as an attractive proposition to work with.

Brands want to see engagement. Having a thriving community around your blog will make it stand out to other readers, but also to PR companies and brands. They will see your content as valuable as it's creating great engagement. Your community can help you generate this positive impression to the outside world. Which in turn helps to attract brands and future community members.

How do you even start building an epic community?

Over the years I've figured out a few key things that have helped me build my community and also things that I see working really well for others too.

Let's start with the most important. Be yourself and be flawed. People desire human interaction, so they connect with 'real' characters. Increasingly online people are craving the people they follow to be 'real' and show they're human. There seems to be a never-ending supply of entrepreneurs and influencers lazing around on yachts or sipping Mai Tais on the beach. Talking about their epic seven-figure launches. This is getting really old. People are craving *'real'*.

Sharing yourself in this way gives many potential points of resonance with your ideal reader, who will, over time become a super fan of yours, if you're lucky. When you speak, they will connect with your words. They have more opportunity to think, 'me too' when watching your videos or reading your content. It's these points of resonance which build into a relationship.

Remember, people buy from, or remember, people they know, like and trust. For me, even now, I feel as if I'm still putting more of myself into my content than before. It wasn't that I was intentionally holding back at the start, but it can take time to really step into who you are online, and confidence plays a huge part in this too.

Can you show up as your true flawed self?

Showing you're flawed is so important. None of us live shiny perfect lives in reality. While I'm not suggesting you turn into 'Negative Nelly', people want to see the real you. They want to know how things 'really' are. If I'm having a bad day, I'll give myself time to wallow and feel what I'm feeling, then I'll pick myself up and get on with it.

Another reason people are often reluctant to share themselves fully if they know it will polarise their audience. Some people will like them and some will dislike them. They're afraid to turn people off. However, remember what I said earlier in this book. To attract your true fans, you're going to repel others and that's OK. You're not for everyone. No-one is! If you feel as if you don't want to express an opinion in case you turn people off, then you're not being true to yourself.

What we focus on is what we get. For example, I once did a Facebook live moments after I'd left my daughter crying at school. I told my audience I was a little off kilter, explained why and said I would try to get my energy back. People appreciate your honesty and they love you more for sharing your real life with them.

A great friend of mine who I've already mentioned in this book, Katy, is a true example of how being 'real' can and will create a shift in your business. Katy is a wonderful blogger, who admits to having lost her way on occasions during her blogging journey. She felt as if she was trying to do what everyone else was doing. Creating great content for her YouTube channel, but frustratingly not getting the traction she hoped for.

One day when feeling a bit fed up of the fakery she was seeing online. She vlogged about her cluttered home and decided to go on a mission to declutter her entire house and share all of it, messy cupboards and all on her YouTube channel. She showed the piles of mess, the bin bags, the stuff *everywhere*. She spoke of her feelings and of the systems as she was using to get rid of all of these possessions. The reaction? People LOVED it.

Her viewers grew and grew. More and more people joined her Facebook group asking for tips and sharing how they loved how real and honest she was. She wasn't trying to be anyone else. She just showed up as her real true, flawed self and her audience *found her.* We're all flawed, no-one is perfect, and we definitely shouldn't try to be. You might even find that projecting 'perfection' can be off-putting. People won't feel as if you could be their friend. They will see you as untouchable.

It's nice (and business savvy) to be nice

Being a nice helpful person should never be underestimated. Human kindness goes a long way to help build relationships. When building any business, people can get a little hung up on the strategy. Causing us to leave the human interaction aspects by the wayside.

However, it's this kindness which will set you apart from the millions of other bloggers out there. I believe this is part of the reason why I've been successful, because I ALWAYS give value. People know that they will get something from my posts/challenges/courses. Go out of your way to help others, even if there's nothing directly in it for you right now. You will be creating goodwill, which is priceless.

Engage with your audience

Your content is a great place to start building your community. Make sure you ask questions at the end of your blog posts and in your social media statuses. People love giving their opinion and your audience will be no different. You can also use Facebook groups to engage with your audience or other people in your niche. It's so important to just make connections without the constant need for promotion. Ask easy questions and then interact with people who comment.

If someone takes the time to email you to thank you for something you've put out there, then always respond. Then take the time to go and follow them on social media and interact with them there. This will help you build us a relationship with a fan who is loving what you are creating right now.

> Don't just focus on getting new readers. Make sure you're looking after the readers you have too.

ABY'S ACTION STEP

Make sure you've added your blog to your personal profile on Facebook. If people want to connect with you after interacting with you in a Facebook group, they will be able to connect with you on your blog or join your community. It's about building proper connections and being of service to other people. Trust that they will value your expertise and they will find you (if you have your profile set up correctly!).

Transition them to the list!

Remember this: Your email list is the only list of subscribers that you actually **own**.

When I started blogging I was like a sponge. I wanted to consume everything I could and learn as much as I could pack in my head. However, no-one was talking about email lists? I remember being focused on growing my social media followers. No-one mentioned an email list to me. None of the conferences I went to had sessions on list building and, at least, within UK bloggers I hadn't seen anyone blogging about it either. I will always regret not starting to focus on building my email list sooner.

The more people you have on your email list the better, as long as they are engaged. Vanity numbers won't help you at all, in fact, it will end up costing you. If people feel part of the community they will want to take a step further and join your list. You can then develop a deeper relationship with them via your emails. Getting people's email list is like getting into their inner sanctum. You can communicate with them when you want and that communication isn't preyed to changing algorithms.

Picture the scene… You go to a party (read - meet people on Instagram or Facebook). You make a connection with them, but then you try to take them home (sell them a product or ask them to be a super fan). Woah there! It's WAY too soon! You need to date them first and build a relationship. That's done by getting them on your email list. This allows you to nurture the relationship and give value beyond what they see on social media. Then you will be in a better position to sell your products or for them to become a raving fan of yours.

Be their everything

Become their go-to source of information in a particular niche. Produce awesome content; that should go without saying, but I'm sure somewhere along the line we have all published something that wasn't our best work. Why not focus on making sure that the content you post is epic? Add videos, downloads, graphics, the works. Create a post that makes people want to follow you everywhere, as they know they will get value.

Be consistent with your content creation. If you can only produce one awesome post a week, then do that, but deliver what you say you will EVERY WEEK.

Learn what your audience needs and give it to them. To do this you need to spend time in groups listening to people's issues and problems. Make notes of exactly how they articulate these worries and problems. This means you will be able to use their exact words in your blog posts. They will feel as if you're talking directly to them. Interview some audience members so you get a better understanding of how your content could help them.

Pat Flynn from Smart Passive Income has a multi-million-pound business and an email list of 200k people. Yet he still takes the time to interview ten people from his list each month to find out their current issues, problems, and concerns. This will then help him shape his content to match their needs.

Respond to comments

When you first start out it's so important to respond to blog comments, social media comments, and emails. As your blog grows this might not be sustainable; but do it while you can. Responding to people helps you to develop a much stronger connection. I really believe my blog and my profile grew quickly in the early years because I responded to EVERYTHING. People knew I was accessible, helpful and nice!

Now that my blog has grown, and the number of messages/comments has grown too, I don't have enough time to get around everything. But when your blog is smaller and you can, you definitely should do it. Not everyone will go back to see your comment, BUT the next reader will see it and they will be more likely to comment if they see you respond to your audience. Thank people for stopping by, for retweeting, for sharing your Facebook posts. Respond to questions and emails. It will make the difference.

Another method you could consider is to host a linky. This is an online party where bloggers link up a certain type of post to the hosts blog. Linkys are a great way to immerse yourself in the community and also develop your own community. You can either host it alone or co-host with a blogging friend. I've done both and there are positives and negatives with each.

TOP TIP

Don't make the topic of you linky too specific or tricky, people haven't got the time for that. Make it easy to join in with, so it becomes a no-brainer. Although the linky badge links are no-follow, they are still links and you'll be working to build a community around your blog. Other people will then find you through the posts that people are linking up.

It takes time to run a linky, but remember in life **you either pay with your money or your time. There's no other way.** You can use money to pay for ads, or hire help or pay for schedulers, or you pay with your time and do it all yourself. For example, if you want a free social media scheduler, you will end up paying with your time, as these won't be as efficient as the paid for services. **Nothing is ever free**

Feature other bloggers

There are so many ways you can do this. You could write a curated round up post (for example, '10 Instagram feeds I love'). Or a crowd sourced post and ask the community for their thoughts on a topic, including them with links to the blogs. The bloggers will feel included and will share the post, further widening your community. Posts like this are also super quick to write, which is important for us busy mamas.

Learn about your community & connect with them

If you can't help someone in your audience with their problem, then be the connector. Take time to learn about people in your community, so you can suggest who else in the community they should chat to or connect with. For example, if someone asks about Blogger (the platform) in my community, then I hold my hands up as I know nothing about Blogger. However, I do that one of my group, Morgan, is on Blogger and that she's super helpful, so I tag her. I might not be able to directly help, but I listen, learn and know who can help them. Maybe, it's just realising two community members have things in common and shouting out that they should have a chat. Even if you can't help personally, you can still build a community around your blog by being the connector.

Start a hashtag or a monthly challenge

You could start a hashtag community. Amy and I started #LittleFierceOnes and it now has hundreds of thousands of images in the gallery. When we first launched it we would feature contributors on our blogs and on our Instagram feeds. This is a great way build a community around your blog, especially in the early days. You could host a challenge. I've done a few five-day challenges – Project Productivity, The Wrap Party, Let's Get Visible, Ignite Your Audience and they are fabulous for building connections and community. Or maybe you could consider an ongoing project, such as Project 365 where you take a photograph every day for a year.

Reward loyalty

Try rewarding community members by shouting them out on social media or feature them in groups. For example, when I ran 'The List Linky' I would shout out six people each week. They would get a backlink from a 51 DA (Domain Authority) blog, which was a boost to their SEO. I would also retweet their posts when they join AND share directly on Twitter as well. In my Facebook group, I shout-out to the top engaged (like two-four) people each week. They then get a shout-out in the group and I'll tweet something out for them to highlight their blog. I have a big audience that they can tap into as a reward for being a valuable member of my community. You could give your community special perks or promote them in other ways on your platform. Whatever form it takes for you, always show that you're grateful to your community.

Build your blog on a single powerful idea

Although this idea might change and evolve over the months and years, as you progress in your blogging journey, it's so important to get to the core desire of the people you're trying to help. One way to do this is to ask 'so that'. For example, I teach mums to turn their blog into a biz. [so that] they can give up their job [so that] they can have more freedom [so that] they can be with their kids. Therefore, the core desire is not having a business or even making money, it's gaining the freedom to be with their kids. If you help people to become vegetarian, what are those people's core desire? They want to stop eating meat [so that] they can be healthier [so that] they feel better within themselves, for example.

Let your readers have input into your content plan

You can survey them or poll in a Facebook group. Often what you think will be their biggest issue, isn't. So, it's great practice to check and make sure you can write content to help their immediate needs. If you have a couple of ideas, ask them to choose which they want to read/watch next. For example, you want to write a post about vegan menu planning, why not ask your audience which they struggle with more, vegan breakfasts or lunches. This can then help to shape your content, so it's perfect for your audience's current need.

ABY'S ACTION STEP

Grab a notebook and brainstorm how you are going to start developing a community around your blog. Then get to work!

You must have clarity as a leader

One of the biggest problems I see with bloggers who are trying to 'make it' is their lack of clarity. You need clarity around what you do and what you can offer. If you aren't clear people will not follow you and you will not be able to develop a strong community. If you think, 'well, I'll write about a bit of everything' and you will project that, 'jack of all trades, master of none' vibe. Consequently, people aren't going to be convinced of the value you offer. It's so important to have clarity and know where your superpowers lie.

For me, I'm good at motivating, figuring out what people should be doing and have first-hand experience of turning a blog to a successful biz (even with PND and a kid hanging off me most of the time). You will have superpowers too. Ask your friends what your superpower is. It's likely to be something you find easy, but other people don't seem to. Often we are 'too British' and hide our light under a bushel. However, you can't build a community around your blog until you know what you're about and where your own strengths lie.

If you don't have this clarity, then you might have to wait until you do. Remember where we started, every mass movement has a charismatic leader, a future driven cause and offers their followers a vehicle for change. You can't offer any of this without clarity. Your potential followers want to be as clear in their lives, as you are in yours. So get clear.

Community is EVERYTHING

Helping your community is vital

Now you might be thinking why would I want to help fellow bloggers? Surely they're my competition... Why would I want to help them? I think there are people who actually believe this, which is sad and the blogging fairies will NOT be sprinkling blogging fairy dust over those particular people. Supporting other bloggers can actually help you and your blog too.

Most of this support comes down to good karma, put in the work helping others and you know what? They will be more inclined to help you in return.

Do you remember the person who you tweet and who never responds? Nope, you will be too busy with the people who do respond. The person you retweet and support, yet they never retweet for you? The person that never responds to the comments you leave on their blog; will you keep visiting and commenting? I'm guessing probably not. You see, this blogging thing is reciprocal, you get out what you put in.

Apart from banking on the law of reciprocity, you should want to help other bloggers because it is a nice thing to do! There needs to more kindness in the world and we can make an impact today, right in our own backyard. If you help solely to be helped, then you're probably in for a disappointment. If you help from a genuine place, then you will benefit in spades. In real life, you would tell a friend about a great book you read. Sure you would! So, tell the world about a great blog post you read too! This mutual support really does make the community a nicer place.

There's no doubt that helping fellow bloggers will help you build your own tribe. As I'm constantly stating, hands down the best thing to come out of blogging for me has been the friendships. True, long-lasting, genuine friendships, what could be better? By building a tribe you're also eliminating some of the loneliness which can often rear its head when you begin to work from home.

A simple retweet or share could open the door for a larger collaboration in the future. You never know what could happen. This is one of the most wonderful things about blogging. You never know what's going to happen next!

There are so many ways that you can highlight other bloggers and share the love. From sharing or commenting on their content to offering to help them resolve an issue they have or even featuring them in your own content. What matters is that we all take time to support each other.

Collaboration is key.

Collaborate

One of the things I love the most about blogging is collaborating with other bloggers. Most of the time we work on our own, so it can be wonderful to work with others. There are so many benefits and equally as many forms that collaborations can take.

Why collaborate?

Firstly, working with others is usually more fun than going solo. I also find it is really useful to have another blogger as a sounding board. Friends who don't blog will never be able to offer the same insight that another blogger will.

We can ALL learn from so much from others wherever we are in this journey. Collaborations can help us see things from another person's viewpoint too.

Diving into a collaboration is a wonderful way to get to know other bloggers or strengthen existing friendships.

You can inspire and motivate each other and together you can make more of an impact, than you will be able to make solo.

If you are thinking of working together and approaching brands, you will find that you are able to pitch a bigger brand than you would be able to pitch alone. As your combined stats will be much more desirable.

Together we are stronger.

You will both increase your readership, gaining exposure to each other's audience. This collaboration will expand the community around your blog and may even increase opportunities offered to you.

How do you find bloggers to work with?

You might already have a 'tribe' or a list of people who you would immediately want to work with. However, if you don't, here are some tips on how you could start a potential collaboration.

You first need to identify the bloggers that you would like to work with. These could be in your niche or maybe in a complimentary one. This decision depends on what you hope to achieve from the collaboration. You might find them in the blogs you read, or maybe on social media. The next step is to talk to them. I know! For those of you who are introverts, stepping out of our shells can be tricky, but just start engaging with their posts, chat on social media. Just get to know them.

When you feel the time is right, pitch them your idea. You might be nervous, but chances are they will be flattered that you have asked to work with them. If it's a no, don't take it personally. We all have lots of stuff competing for our time and it just might not be a good fit in that moment.

Drawing a blank? Need some collaboration ideas?

There are lots of ways that bloggers can work with each other:

- An interview series. This is quite easy to do and doesn't take either party too much time. All you have to do it send your collaborators a list of questions and some guidelines, that's it really. Then when the interview is live on your blog, they will help to share it on social media giving you exposure to their audience. They, in turn, get exposure to yours.
- Run a feature series. Pick a theme i.e. party planning and everyone involved writes a post on one aspect, you can then all link to each other, or post one a day and link on to the next person's blog post.
- A 'one-off' double whammy. Both bloggers create a post based on a theme or a certain topic. They then post it on the same day or within the same week and both link to and help to publicise each other's posts. One post written, but double the exposure. You could even do a part one and part two?
- Recommend each other. Why not recommend each other to your readers and the brands you work

with. If you do a sponsored post, ask the brand if they're looking for more bloggers and if they are pass your collaborator's name on. I have a few people that I always recommend to brands I work with. The brand will love you for it, trust me. It saves them time searching for good bloggers. I also recommend other bloggers to event organisers.

- Run a linky together. Over the years I've run five linkys all with other bloggers at some point. Linky's can be great you tap into new audiences and divide the workload. It's also more fun!

- Start a collaborative blog. Why not join together are write a blog? You might choose to cover things you feel you can't on your solo blog.

- Comment on each other's posts and social media updates. Join each other's email lists, mutually like and share each other's social media updates. To keep on track, you can use Twitter lists and you can even choose to be notified if your collaborators post to Instagram to help keep you up to date. This REALLY helps them out and you too!

- Twitter chats can be a great way to collaborate and they are often a great way to gain exposure too.

- Why not allow another blogger to guest post on your blog. They will then help to promote their post on social media and expose your blog to their audience.

- Guest appearances. You could also post on someone else's blog yourself. This is fab for SEO, as the piece will include a link to your blog. You will also reach their audience.

- Join together to run a giveaway a larger prize and have your giveaway reach a large audience.

- Write roundups. These can take so many forms. Sharing your favourite bloggers in a post, or top blogs in a certain area. If you don't know your collaborators, then a '5 new blogs' roundup might be a possibility.
- Set up a Facebook group, in which you can share ideas and ask questions.
- Actually work together. If you live near enough, why not work with each other. You could alternate houses or even meet in a coffee shop.
- Attend events together. The other person will introduce you to people they know, and you can return the favour. It's great to have moral support too.
- Host a contest. Maybe you could run a post a picture contest on Instagram.
- Throw a Pin it party. Invite guest pinners to add content on a particular board at a chosen time
- You could collaborate on platforms such as YouTube, Facebook or even on a podcast. They all offer awesome possibilities to reach your combined audience.
- Share your knowledge and co-create books, eBooks, workbooks.
- Hold each other accountable. This is a great way to collaborate and help each other to stay on track of your goals and workload. Share your ideas and keep each other updated.
- Create a course or run a webinar. Do you have the knowledge or a skill to share? You could teach together, either online or a physical workshop.

- Produce physical products. There are lots of products that bloggers, especially those with a flair for design could produce to sell.
- Blog newsletters. You could create a co-written email and then include each other's opt-in link.

Hopefully, that will have got your juices flowing. Collaborations can be amazing, so get stuck in!

ABY'S ACTION STEP

Divide a piece of paper into two columns. On the left side write down all the people you would like to collaborate with and on the right write down all the different ways that you could collaborate with that person. Then approach them and pitch your ideas.

CHAPTER 12

Getting social.

If you want to be a successful blogger, then you need some sort of social media strategy. There's no point in writing away and posting like fury if no-one knows you're there. With so many social media platforms it can simply be overwhelming to learn how to use all of them fully and effectively.

In my first eighteen months of blogging, I grew my social following from zero to over 15k, with almost 8.5k being followers on Twitter.

In order to establish authority and trust on social media, it's very important to write a professional sounding social media bio for your profiles. When someone finds your account and is deciding whether or not to start following you, or whether to follow your suggestions to buy X product, one of the first things they will do is to check your profile to see what you're all about. Then they make up their mind based almost entirely on your bio, so you better make sure it sounds professional and compelling.

Brevity is key on social media as you often don't have masses of space to play with. Your bio is just an introduction, a snippet that reflects the most important information you want people to know about you. It needs to be compelling and includes a call to action, but it certainly shouldn't be War and Peace!

Remember you're trying to attract customers, network or otherwise build a reputation, so you should make sure to use a professional tone. Some of your personality thrown in for good measure will give people something to remember you by. After all, social media is personal in nature.

Make sure you avoid using lots of jargon and buzz words. Your objective is not to sound clever. Just to be clear and sum up what it is that you do and who you help. Don't dress it up with buzzwords which might be confusing to others. Less is more, so be frugal with your use of words, especially if there's a word limit.

If you're still having a hard time finding your 'tone' then imagine your ideal customer avatar and keep them in mind when you're writing. Maybe you even know someone in real life who fits into the right demographic. If so, imagine you're writing for them.

You can use targeted hashtags in your bio to both show what you do and make your bio appear in search results. Depending on your industry/niche it might be appropriate to include some emoticons. These can add fun and emphasis to your bios and also they can be used instead of words. They take up less characters than words, so can be useful.

Mention *relevant* accomplishments and significant awards to stand out from the masses (no-one needs to know that you won a prize for playing the trumpet when you were at school!).

As always, being authentic online matters and your bios are no exception. Write in the first person and just be genuine, it will make you seem like a real person and not just a social media profile. Any potential follower will be thinking, 'Why should I follow her?'. So show them how will it benefit them.

The link in your bio should ideally be used to get people to opt-in to your mailing list. Do this by directing them to your free product or download. This is more effective than just asking them to visit your site.

Being original can sometimes be tricky, but you need to try to avoid following the crowd to make your bio stand out. Depending on your character and the industry you work in you could add in some humour to make your bios engaging, even Hilary Clinton did this!

Still struggling? Don't worry, not everyone is a born bio writer and that's fine. Hiring a professional to write your bio shouldn't be expensive and it will result in a much more professional sounding and engaging experience for your visitors. You might be able to find someone who can do this for you on Fiverr or a similar site.

Let's dig into social media strategy

Social media is an incredibly powerful tool and you need to learn how to harness the platforms relevant to you. Preferably, without going mad or drowning under a huge workload. It can be difficult to keep on top of everything, which is why you need a solid strategy.

Twitter

Twitter is a high volume/low value network. It's fast-moving and you need to know how to get it to work for you, or it will pass you by. Your strategy here should be quantity; aim for multiple tweets a day (even of the same piece of content). Due to the speed of the feed if you're just sending out a couple of tweets a day, they are simply going to be swallowed up.

You NEED Twitter lists. Without them, Twitter may well be overwhelming and you will probably end up losing track of everything. You could have a list for your blog (those you interact with), closer friends, brands you work with and brands you want to work with. The possibilities are endless!

Now this is the key. Schedule, schedule, schedule. It's so important to schedule tweets that share your post links. If you don't, you can bet your bottom dollar someone else is and your one tweet will get lost in the noise. I know people worry about flooding other people's feeds. However, I believe that people follow so many accounts, that there's always a mixed flow of information on follower's timelines.

I use Social Oomph to schedule which, in my opinion, is the best scheduler and it saves me hours of inputting for a very small fee. There are so many other options though if you want to try something else. There are a few studies which have looked into the best times to tweet, but I really think it's best to test times out with your own audience and go from there. Remember, if you have a following in another time zone you will need to have your tweets going out 24 hours a day to cover the time differences.

When I started to build my following, I would go into the profiles of people I followed and go down their following list. I would simply follow those who caught my eye. At the start, I would unfollow people who didn't follow back, as you were then limited to following 2k until your follower number built up. I retweet when I could and use my lists to make it easy for me to retweet posts shared by members of my tribe.

Personally, I schedule every new post of my own personal content to go out once every eight hours, twenty times. Every review or sponsored post will go out once every eight hours, ten times. My evergreen posts go out less frequently, but on an ongoing basis.

Responding to tweets is really important and can really help you grow your follower numbers. I try to respond to every tweet I'm mentioned in. Occasionally, my feed goes mad meaning I may miss one or two. I do try to thank people for retweeting/sharing my posts, mainly because it's just good manners!

Using the #FF (Follow Friday) hashtag is a lovely way to show your appreciation to other bloggers and businesses you work with. It can help to build your followers too.

Hashtags help people who aren't following you find your posts, so it would be silly not to use them if you want to increase your readership. One or two per post is fine, don't go crazy!

Regardless of who follows you, I think you should only follow people back if their profile interests you. Otherwise, it just seems inauthentic and your feed will become too difficult to manage. I don't unfollow people who don't follow me, mainly because I never check. However, you can use a variety of sites to monitor your unfollowers if you want to go down that route. It's more important to pay attention to this when you're limited in your numbers of allowed followers.

Facebook

Facebook is a tricky platform. Frequent algorithm changes mean it can be difficult to get traction without paying for adverts. It's a low volume/high value network. Lots of updates will make people feel bombarded and will probably annoy them. This network moves slower, therefore, you need to make each post count. As with everything, there's varying advice as to the number of updates you should post to your page each day. However, the focus should always be on the quality of content and engagement it garners.

Liking and commenting on your blog's Facebook page can make your page more visible. In terms of the content you share try to mix it up. Share any interesting work of others that you think your audience will enjoy, mixed in with your own content.

To find this content; read blogs, look at your Facebook feed and share interesting stories from businesses you support. I use the save function on Facebook to keep all of the things I might want to re-share in one handy place. Also look through the Explore feed, saving anything that's relevant to your audience and that's doing well over there.

Again, as for Twitter, I truly believe testing posting at different times and seeing how *your* audience reacts is the best way. Personally, I schedule my blog posts to appear on my page at 8.00 am and they're shared there just once initially. I might then share the evergreen ones again at some point in the future. You can pop them on a spreadsheet to make rescheduling them easier.

The key for Facebook is to create genuine engagement and not simply use it to drop links in order to get traffic back to your blog. Remember, Facebook really want people to stay on Facebook. So, the reach of posts with links taking people away from Facebook will be less than those without. You can try different ways to engage with your audience, asking your audience questions is a great start. If people like your status you can then invite them to like your page.

The more a post is liked, the more people Facebook will show it too. Therefore, if you have a tribe, get them to like and comment on your updates. This should help you see a rise in the number of people seeing the post.

Facebook groups are amazing and can be used in so many different ways. If you have a product or service, you could create a group for those people — for example, I've had groups for people on my free challenges and courses. Groups like this are a wonderful way to provide further support to your clients. There are Facebook groups for EVERYTHING, so you're sure to find one which is perfect for you and your needs. Make sure you are joining the right groups. If you're researching your market you don't want the group to be filled with peers, but rather, you want it filled with people similar to your ideal reader.

Obviously, peer groups are so useful too for other reasons. Joining groups full of likeminded peeps can be so influential in helping you to advance your blog. Whatever niche you're in, you could consider creating a networking group.

Every time you join a group, take a few minutes to introduce yourself to the other members. You're in there to network, so don't just join and lurk. You also don't know what potential opportunities are in the group, so start as you mean to go on. To make it easier, write a bio introducing yourself and your blog, save it and then you can just copy and paste to save time. I have a few versions of mine saved in Airtable.

You can find out so much information about your target audience from Facebook groups; your own and those of others. If you have a topic in mind that you need to research. Join an appropriate group, then use the search box of the side of the group page to search for specific words within that group. Bingo! You will find all of the related posts. This means you can find the specific worries, concerns and pain points of your potential audience so you know exactly what content to create. Make yourself useful and take an active part in the group. Help people and give them the benefit of your experience.

Facebook groups can be pivotal in helping you to make amazing connections with people outside of your niche. Establishing expertise in Facebook groups is such a great way for you to show people that you know your stuff. Establishing the credibility necessary to push your blog to the next level.

Groups can be an effective way to gain valuable feedback. This can either be a secret group with some clients, members of your team or peers, or a larger open group. Creating a VIP group to reward your clients might suit your business model. Make them feel valuable and special. You could use the group to give them exclusive offers and content.

Facebook Live

I remember how sick I felt before I did my first Facebook Live. Oh, I was so worried! I'd been asked to 'go live' in a fellow entrepreneur's Facebook group to talk about productivity. I wondered what I was even doing accepting, but it was too late, I had to go through with it. I'm so glad I did, as about halfway into my *live*, I fell in love with live streaming. There's nothing like 'going live' to enable you to connect in real-time with your audience. You can pick your favourite platform to go live on, as the facility is available on YouTube and Instagram too.

Instagram

Instagram used to be my favourite social network. I grew my larger account reasonably quickly and at one point was getting rapid growth on the platform. A few algorithm changes later and Instagram has definitely fallen out of favour for me. Consistency and engagement is so important. The more you put into the network in terms of engagement, the more you will be rewarded.

Mixing up your hashtags and not just copying the same block of hashtags over and over will help you pick up more likes. Also, make sure you're spreading out your posts to increase your visibility. Posting four images in a row is likely to annoy your followers and lead to unfollows. I often like every post on my feed, it takes milliseconds to double tap and it gives everyone a boost. People may also reciprocate.

Instagram Stories

There's no doubt that having a live 'real' connection with your audience is vital to the success of your blog. People want to have relationships with authentic people, so this live connection is becoming increasingly important.

Google+

Similar to Facebook in that it's a low volume/high value network. Google+ seems to have fallen out of favour with bloggers. I must admit it's a platform that I've never really focused on at all. All I do is auto share my new blog posts. Every time you post on G+ you give google more keywords and information to index and link back to you.

Pinterest

Pinterest is a high volume/high value network. Rather than a social network, it's actually a search engine. You need to post frequently to get noticed in the volume of pins, but the quality of your pins also matters. Use beautiful images, catchy titles and carefully chosen keywords to give yourself the best chance on Pinterest.

When deciding what to pin, think, 'is this content helpful?'. The posts which tend to do well on Pinterest are how tos, tutorials and posts that are giving the reader useful information. Think will someone want to repin it and save it to refer back to?

Pin more of other people's content, then of your own. Make sure you're using a headshot for your profile picture as people want to pin from real people. However, when it comes to actual pin design, a pin is 23% more likely to be repinned if the image is NOT someone's face (Curalate research).

Descriptions of your pins are so important and often are the deciding factor when a person is deciding whether to click through and read your post. Use positive words like fantastic, awesome, but also practical, descriptive key words. Make this description enticing. The average pin in repinned ten times, compared to the average tweet which is retweeted only 1% of the time (Piqora).

Make sure you're rearranging your boards seasonally, so your popular ones or the current seasonal boards are at the top.

Linked In

This network is low volume/high value professional network. This would be the place to post your more formal, professional, technical content around your sector, i.e., for me, it would be blogging posts.

Share your content to your timeline and in any relevant groups you belong to. Make the most of your banner image by sharing what you do, possibly directing people to your opt-in.

Your bio needs to be focused on who you help and how you help them. For example, mine is *'Helping Mum Bloggers turn their blogs into biz's to give them more freedom - Clear roadmap - Courses - Membership'.*

Then expand on this with a powerful 'Summary', which is also the place to place your opt-in link.

Wrapping up social

A general tip would be to make sure your social media buttons are in a prominent place on your sidebar of your blog. I also put them at the bottom of every post, with sharing buttons. Make it really easy for people to follow you and share your posts on a variety of networks.

If you want to grow your social media accounts, then you should be actively looking for new ways to get extra followers. The more followers you get, the larger the number of people that each of your new posts will be automatically broadcast to. This is ultimately one of the primary objectives of social media and it's what will give you a lot more reach and authority. Thus, ensuring that all your hard work pays off.

One of the simplest and easiest ways to get more followers on any platform is to head onto your platform of choice and then start following people. Keep in mind the types of people who you want to engage with. Make sure you're not just following anyone; remember you want them to engage with your content and vice versa. Otherwise, the numbers you create are simply for vanity.

What you'll find is that a large proportion of those people you add will respond in kind and immediately add you back. It can be slow going, but it's an almost guaranteed way to extend your reach and influence. Go down the rabbit hole and look at the followers of people who you follow or the people these people follow themselves as chances are they will be similar people and might be interesting for you to follow as well.

Retweeting, repining or re-sharing is another great way to grow your following. The people you help will feel the law of reciprocity and will want to help you out. This means you will be exposed to their audience. You could try teaming up with someone else and giving mutual shout-outs to each other's audiences.

If you have an audience already then make sure you leverage that opportunity. For example, ask your blog readers to follow you on Twitter. Your YouTube audience to check you out on Facebook. Most importantly try to get them all onto your list!

This sounds like a catch-22, but the more followers you have, the more followers you will continue to gain. The reason for this is simple: people like to follow accounts that look popular; social proof strikes again! Once you build up your follow numbers, momentum kicks in, meaning often the growth will become easier than it was at the start.

ABY'S ACTION STEP

Take some time now to map out your social media strategy. Where are you going to focus your efforts? Which platform are you going to focus on? Where do your ideal readers spend their time? What sort of content are you going to create there? How will you generate engagement?

CHAPTER 13

'You're so lucky.' The truth behind success.

Blogging has given us so much. The opportunities have been totally wonderful. Countless holidays, press trips abroad, wonderful events and amazing products. I've reached the Brilliance in Blogging finals multiple times and now have the means of being more financially secure than I've ever been previously. I've spoken at conferences and have even been paid to do a commercial photoshoot.

Personally, on a base level, my blog still gives me somewhere to escape to when the daily stresses leave me needing to retreat for a while.

Over the years, I've had so many people tell me I'm lucky.

Lucky…?

My blog is my hobby and my livelihood. It's important for my mental well-being, but also to pay the bills. I've had many comments over the years saying that I'm so lucky to get the opportunities I do through my blog. I'm so grateful for every opportunity I've had *believe me.* I really am, but largely I'm NOT lucky. The opportunities I get are through sheer hard work and an unbelievable number of hours clocked in. Not luck, believe me, it's pure graft. I remain thankful and I'm truly BLESSED to do something I love every day. Luck it is not.

The truth about being successful

Being successful isn't easy; it rarely happens overnight and especially within blogging it is HARD WORK. Seriously… HARD WORK.

I've read many comments recently from people wanting to start blogging to make instant money. This makes my blood boil. The thought of anyone blogging purely to make money makes me sad. Yes, we all have to earn a living, but I believe our primary reason for blogging should be because we love to blog or, like me, '*have*' to blog.

How do you become successful? Well, first things first, you have to say it like you mean it. "I will be successful," that's it, stop there. No qualifier, just that, 'I will be successful.' Then you MAKE IT HAPPEN.

"As you think, so shall you become." - Bruce Lee

Some of reading this may already be making excuses. You have so many commitments, maybe a lack of support; but here's the thing, it's hard for *everyone*. No-one has the monopoly on juggling the balls. We're all doing it, every. single. day. I often work until 1.00 am. It doesn't make me a better blogger than you if you don't, it just means that I'm more committed (and maybe a little obsessed…).

Achieving your goals is hard work and takes a lot of dedication, commitment and focus. The reason many people fail is that they lack this focus and commitment. You can be the best writer and photographer, but if you aren't prepared to make sacrifices, you will not achieve the success you desire. This might sound harsh. Maybe it is, but it's also the truth.
You don't get credit for having a tough time. You get credit for making things happen regardless of your circumstances.

Everyone has problems to overcome and their own mountains to climb.

Making a success of anything is tough. If you don't want to make sacrifices, I would guess that means you don't want the end result enough. Which is fine, but then you need to let go of the idea you will make a success of it and love it for what it is.

There are so many reasons why making a success of your blog can be tough. Maybe you work full-time, have a baby keeping you up all night or have young kids running around. These are problems for sure, but they are not necessarily bigger or more difficult to overcome than anyone else's problems.

Whatever your personal situation is and whatever you are striving for, you have to push to make it happen. You have to push when you don't feel like it. When you would rather be with your family, chilling with your partner, sleeping, doing anything rather than working. The fact is that these are the sacrifices you will sometimes have to make to make a success of your online dream.

Sure you might not have to sacrifice anything and eventually over time, your blog might pick up and make money. However, to reach your goals quickly and achieve success you need to push, graft and sacrifice *some* of the time.

I work late at night, grabbing time wherever I can during the day. My way might not work for you. Your kids might be better sleepers than mine, so it might work for you to wake up before them to have some time to focus on work. Whatever makes it work for you. The thing is if you want your blog to be your full-time business, you have to treat it like a business NOW. We can do AMAZING things when we put our minds to it.

'What we focus on expands'. - T. Harv Eker

You need to LOVE what you do

There's no way you will have the strength to make this happen if you don't absolutely love what you do. FACT. If you think your blog is nothing more than a way to earn money, I wouldn't go down this road as it will never be the thing that makes you happy. You need to love your blog regardless of the money it does or doesn't make you. That shines through to your readers and that keeps you going when you are burning the midnight oil.

Being successful takes a bucket load of commitment

The reality of making your blog work isn't glamorous. If you're juggling a full-time job as well, the reality is probably getting up an hour or two earlier and working before you leave for work. See, I told you it wasn't glamorous. Then again, running your own business isn't 9.00 am – 5.00 pm either... Creating the life you want takes all of these things; hard work, commitment and sometimes sacrifice, but it IS worth it all. Ten times over.

You'll have to ditch perfection

We all want to get things right and do the very best job we can, but don't over analyse every aspect of what you do. It's more important to make progress. Get those posts written, not perfect.

'Take imperfect action'

Chances are every time you read a post you could make small changes, but publishing great engaging content is more important. Perfection isn't a useful state to be seeking. You will probably fail at some point, EVERYONE does. Some things will work well, while others not so much. The key is to learn from the failures and KEEP GOING.

Visualise your dream future

When things go wrong don't use it as an excuse to bail. Things will go wrong, that's life. Collaborations may not go your way, but if you visualise how you want your future to be, these are just bumps in the road. Bumps you're very capable of navigating. Be creative, add value, strive to do better and you will *become* better.

ABY'S ACTION STEP

In three years' time, you are living out your goal. Envision yourself in that moment. What are you doing? Who is with you? What are you wearing? What's around you? How do you feel? What was your favourite moment of that day? Who do you have to thank for helping you get to this point? What is the best advice you could give someone to achieve what you have? What is the biggest compliment someone could give you? Why do you feel so complete?

Wouldn't it be great if we could see into the future and live today with the added benefit of hindsight and experience? Having that sort of information would make it so much easier to make our decisions and be confident about our plans.

It can be so hard to know which direction to head in and super difficult not to get bogged down by the daily 'stuff'. Not really knowing if this 'stuff' is contributing to us moving forward or not.

Your luck is in, as I want to share my experience with you and give you a peek inside my head. Hopefully, letting you in on the things I wish I'd known at the start of my blogging journey, will help you fast-track your own success. Saving you from some of those bumps in the road!

Summary of my top tips for success

1. Just do it. The blog; something new on there; a collaboration; whatever you're passionate about, just start. You will never feel the time is right. There's never a perfect time. Just take the leap and do it.

2. Your mindset is the most powerful thing you have. Have determination and act like you're already living the life you want to live.

3. Take imperfect action. Done is WAY better than potentially perfect.

4. The number of likes and followers aren't as important as your true fans. One hundred regular dedicated readers are WAY better than 1,000 page views.

5. Try things. You won't know whether something will work until you give it a try.

6. Don't be overwhelmed. You'll learn fast and you will never stop learning.

7. Make your goals a given. You *will* do it. Tell yourself that. You just have to believe it, then you will make it happen.

8. Have faith that you know the answer. Do what lights you up and the rest will work itself out.

9. Being uncomfortable is where the magic happens. Nothing remarkable was ever achieved in the cosiness of your comfort zone.

10. Don't be afraid to ask for help. Invest in yourself to grow personally and to grow your business. Choose the right investments for you.

11. Outsource stuff you don't like doing. You can find people to do these tasks and it doesn't have to cost the earth.

These lessons would have helped me so much, as I was navigating my blog in the early years, so soak them in and let them make a difference to you.

ABY'S ACTION STEP

Which of these points do you feel you can implement immediately in your blog and your life?

CHAPTER 14

What do successful people have in common?

There a few characteristics that most successful people share; being focused and working hard being just two. However, there are habits that we can all learn to adopt which can improve our chances of success in our work lives.

Serve first

I think being a good person goes a long way in this world. I fully believe that helping others makes you a better and more fulfilled person. If they return the favour then that's wonderful, but you should not be giving with any expectation of receiving. Remember it's nice to be nice.

Complete your least favourite tasks first

Do you put things off? Is there one task on your to-do list that you don't really fancy and consequently it's getting lower and lower on your to-do list? You will have a more pleasant day without that task looming over you, so get it done and ticked off. This will change your mind set for the rest of the day.

'If it's your job to eat a frog, it's best to do it first thing in the morning. And if it's your job to eat two frogs, it's best to eat the biggest one first' - Mark Twain

Don't do what you've always done

If you do what you've always done, you will get what you have always got. So, if there's a particular part of your life that you wish was better, CHANGE what you are doing in that area. Look at it with fresh eyes and try something new!

Use the morning to your advantage

If you're an early bird, then don't hit the snooze button, get up and start your day. Do all the tasks you need to get done while the rest of the house sleeps. If you're a perpetual snooze button hitter, STOP IT! Get up as soon as your alarm goes off and before the bed convinces you that just another few minutes will be OK.

Work smarter

This is so important, whatever your day involves, make sure you are being as efficient as possible. Are there any tasks you could automate? Work tasks or personal things like getting the shopping delivered, both would give you more time to spend elsewhere. Be strict with the time you give to tasks and stick to it. Don't get stuck on Facebook all afternoon!

Devise a personal mantra

This might sound a little bit hippyish, but I promise you it can be very powerful. You can have different mantras for different aspects of your life and simply recite them to yourself when needed.

For example, if I am trying to lose weight and struggling to keep motivated I always think, 'A year from now you will wish you started today'. If I'm having a bad day with Ava and tantrums or undesirable behaviour, then I tend to focus on 'This too shall pass'. They can be quotes you have heard, or something more personal to you. What they do is to draw the mind back into focusing on the desired goal and remove it from just reacting.

Celebrate success along the way

It's so important to give yourself a pat on the back as you reach smaller milestones along your journey. Whether you're hoping for weight loss, career success or anything else. Motivate yourself to continue by celebrating your small wins.

Take breaks

Breaks are vital to refresh your mind and remain focused. Without them, your output will drop with your productivity. Even a ten-minute break every hour will be enough to boost your brain and clear your mind.

Believe in yourself

Often this is quite hard, as we tend to be much harder on ourselves than we are on others. The mind is a very powerful thing and self-belief is truly a gift. If your mind is on-side and working with you, not self-sabotaging, then you can achieve anything you set your mind to.

Stay focused

If you're struggling to stay focused in your working life, then you need to close browser windows on your computer. Turn off notifications and really focus on one task at a time. If it's success in a more personal aspect of your life I recommend focusing on the end game and thinking about what your life will be like when you have achieved the success you desire.

Write it down

Writing something down has a very powerful effect. It makes the task seem more concrete and it will help to get your mind focused on your tasks. Oh, and we all love crossing things off a list!

Achieve through modelling

Modelling is a psychological concept where people learn by 'modelling' the behaviour of others. The direction this takes depends on the success you wish to have, but perhaps you could read the success stories of the people who have the success you want; learn from their journey.

Get your mindset right

As a psychology graduate I've spent years studying the power of the mind. The more I've studied, the more I've become totally convinced of the sheer immense power of thought. Success doesn't happen by accident. Successful people create success and a significant amount of this creation is internal. Whether they use positive thought, mantras, visualisation or any other tool. They are imagining it, creating it, and then living it.

Mindset matters... so much!

A success mindset

How do you know if you have the right mindset for success? If you do, how do you make things happen when it feels like the odds are stacked against you and you doubt you will ever be successful?

Let's start by deciding whether any of these statements apply to you:

- You're a creative thinker, who finds solutions to problems.

- You have lots of innovative ideas.

- You have a feeling as if there's something more out there for you.

- You can inspire people to take action.

If any of these statements do ring true for you, chances are you have a growth mindset. This will be a really important asset in your quest to transform your blog into a business.

Creating your success pathway

Taking your blog to the next level and turning it into a thriving business can seem overwhelming. However, there are several steps you can take to make the transition smoother.

One of the most important considerations is to get clear and focused. Having clear goals is so very important. Being specific is not just an option, it's vital. Write down your goal, how you will achieve that goal in smaller steps and then break that list down even further into actionable specific tasks. Then reverse engineering your actions to achieve these goals will help you pave your own success pathway.

Now it's time to take action and make your plan come to life. You need to do more than just simply create a killer plan. Declare aloud what your action steps are. Maybe even get an accountability partner and share with them your goals and plan.

Don't be afraid to delegate tasks, even if you don't have employees yet. Allow family members and friends to help take the load off somewhere else to give you more time to work on your business. Alternatively, if you feel ready you can begin to outsource tasks to a freelancer.

Often in order to create something new, we need to let go of something old. Your home may need to be a little more cluttered or a little less spotless. You may have to let go of a favourite sport or activity for a while, but it's well worth it in the end and it won't be forever.

Keeping your day job is important until you are secure financially in your new business. It may be a difficult to juggle, but creating your own empire is a gift and will be such a reward.

You can make your dreams come true too!

One of my favourite quotes of all time is, *'She believed she could, so she did'*. I love it so much that I'm considering having it tattooed on my wrist. You see, for me, it sums up so much. I have long-since realised the power of the mind on our behaviours and actions. I also realise that most of us barely scratch the surface when utilising this power.

We have endless excuses. I don't have the time. I wish I had more willpower. I have kids. I have a job, as well as my blog. These excuses act as roadblocks which stop us reaching our full potential. It's self-sabotaging behaviour.

The truth is, excluding becoming President, a rocket scientist or maybe a brain surgeon, we can achieve pretty much all we want to, if we totally commit and focus on what we want. The key is, we have to WANT it enough. If we don't, maybe it's someone else's dream that we feel should be ours. We will never strive hard enough or be focused enough to achieve it. You see...

'She believed she could, so she did'

And so can you

Your dreams don't have to be huge, although I think everyone's should be. That's the point of a dream after all! Whatever you wish could come true in your life, you can make it happen by believing in yourself and your ability to do whatever it takes to make it happen.

You see everyday I hear people saying, 'if only I could do this,' 'if only I had more time to do that'. What we need is more focus.

It might be that we're afraid to live our dreams and these excuses come in quite useful. There's nothing like a-get-out-of-jail-card to stop yourself from actually achieving what you want to achieve. Let's not forget it's what YOU want to achieve.

I lost seven stone, how this affects your dreams

You see, I've struggled with my weight my entire life and although I tried many diets and weight loss programs, it always remained a daily struggle. One which I made excuses for on a daily basis. *I was so tired I couldn't do low-calorie. I was going on holiday, so I couldn't diet. I had a conference coming up, so it wasn't a good time.* Maybe I'd lose some weight, start to feel better and convince myself that being I was happy still being overweight. I could almost convince myself I was happy in my own skin. I was just making excuses and I was getting out of jail with them.

Then something changed. With a year until my 40th birthday, I decided that I needed to do this. I WANTED to do this and most of all importantly I realised that I COULD do this. From the end of May 2016 to Christmas 2016, I lost almost seven stone. I lost seven stone, because I believed I could do it for the first time. I have no more willpower than anyone else. I haven't got any miraculous weight loss pills. I've just decided that I could and so I did.

No, it's not easy, but it's totally possible when you commit to making your dreams come true and focus on your dream every day. What I'm trying to say is, don't give up on yourself. Don't let yourself off the hook, because you think it means an easier road ahead. Instead, commit to your dreams and make them happen.

They believed they could, so they did.

How can you change your mindset?

"Success is not the key to happiness. Happiness is the key to success. If you love what you are doing, you will be successful."
- Herman Cain

So, if the biggest influencer of your success is the mindset and you're aware that you have the power within yourself to vastly improve your chances of success.

What happens if you're reading this and already know that you have some mindset issues. You know your mindset needs work, but you're not sure where to start changing the way you think...

One of the easiest ways to do this is to model your behaviour on the mindset of successful people.

What are the habits of successful people?

- Be ruthless in cutting away the things which don't ultimately matter
- Be inspired by others
- Be proactive
- Automate everything they can
- Don't become too accessible
- Work on productivity
- Use breaks effectively to refresh
- Get enough sleep
- Use every second
- Plan/timeline
- Always start with the end in mind
- Embrace change with open arms
- Stay happy
- Take risks
- Be willing to fail
- Use reflection to progress
- Celebrate and champion other people
- Don't give up

- Find a lesson in a mistake
- Touch things once
- Visualise then take action
- Believe it has already happened
- Never stop learning
- Set strategic goals
- Wake up early
- Eat well and value self-care
- Read every day
- Have a great support network
- Delegate almost everything
- Value personal time
- Strive for action, not perfection.
- Don't check emails first thing in the morning
- Have a consistent morning routine
- Give back to community
- Surround themselves with like-minded people
- Accept criticism and move on
- Focus on one thing
- Say no to almost everything
- Use the 80/20 rule (80% of results come from 20% of effort)
- Think win/win

Successful people want success. They're hungry for achievement; they're driven and focused on working towards their end goal. This ensures they take the actions that get them to their desired goals. **They cut the fluff.**

When I think of all the successful people I know one thing stands out that they have all done more than any other action. They **SHOWED UP WITH CONSISTENCY**. They kept going, kept showing up, kept giving value, they kept the faith and you know what it paid off. Success doesn't happen overnight, it takes consistency to start making an impact in the world.

ABY'S ACTION POINT

Make a list of all the characteristics from the above list that you can work on adopting yourself. Changing your natural inclination is not easy, but if you keep your list to hand and repeatedly remind yourself you CAN do it.

How can we use the success of others to be successful ourselves?

Another of my favourite quotes is:

'Comparison is the thief of joy.' - Theodore Roosevelt

However, I want to share with you why you totally SHOULD compare your blog to others. Nope... this is not a typo, I do think we **should** compare our blogs to others, after all it's one of the best sources of learning.

I know most people usually talk about the comparison in a negative way, myself included most of the time. However, I think there are occasions when comparison can actually be a positive tool.

I totally agree that comparing yourself and your accomplishments to other people can be unhealthy. It can make you feel jealous and insecure if you don't handle it a positive way. The key is to handle it the right way. To look at other bloggers and blogs in a professional and objective manner. If you're clever, comparison can actually be a brilliant way to grow as a blogger.

All our lives, we've learned by modelling our behaviour on that of others. It's been that way since we were children. We modelled our behaviour on our parents, our friends, then perhaps our colleagues at work. Then maybe successful people in our field.

You might be wondering how can comparison help you? There are so many ways, let me explain.

You can gain great design inspiration by comparing your blog to one of a more successful blogger in your niche. How do they layout and format their content? Which pages do they have? How do they use colour? Consider all your favourite blogs or successful blogs, do they have a common theme in terms of design? Use this information to feed into your own design. It's not about copying, just getting inspiration for changes you could make and then putting them into practice your way.

Consider the content you see on other blogs. Is there a feature which sparks a fresh idea in you? Are there areas of your own blog that you could expand? What sort of content do you see people engaging with more on other blogs? Maybe this is an area you could cover on your blog. Again, not specific posts, we're talking about general areas here. You can use the flow of traffic to other blogs to identify a demand for content of that sort.

Considering the work others do and the time and effort they put into their blogs can be really useful in giving you a virtual kick up the bum (should you need it!). What are these people doing that is working? Why are they getting the brand work? Now, this doesn't mean you have to replicate everything these people are doing. It's not about copying, simply identifying the characteristics which are leading them to success. This success could be anything you're interested in; perhaps producing helpful content, monetising or doing well on a certain social media channel. Whatever you're looking to improve about your blog.

'If you do what you've always done, you will get what you have always gotten.' - Tony Robbins

You could keep trundling along, doing the same things, hoping that your blog will take off and grow. Or you could look at other blogs to give you a whole heap of ideas and goals. Try something different and be more proactive in your blog's growth. Goal setting is so important!

ABY'S ACTION STEP

Grab your trusty notebook and write down the five blogs you love the most. Ask yourself what are these people doing that you love? Are there any aspects of their blog that you could do without? Is there anything you've listed positive that you could incorporate (your way!) into your own blog? In terms of their audience engagement which content seems to be the most well received? Is your blog lacking in any of these areas? Then try something new. It doesn't matter if it doesn't work the way you thought it might. The important thing is to keep trying.

Do you compare your blog to others? Feel jealousy or do you see ways to grow?

How to overcome jealousy and self-doubt

Do you ever feel disheartened about your blog? Spend time drooling over other people's blogs, so much so that you begin to doubt your own ability? Do you spend a lot of time focused solely on what other people are doing? Yes? You're not alone…

If you have chinks in your self-belief and self-confidence, seeing another blogger killing it can lead to jealousy and even more self-doubt. Within you, you have the power to either spend time focusing on other people or to give all your energy to improving yourself and your own situation.

'What you think about expands. If your thoughts are centred on what's missing, then what's missing by definition, will have to expand' - Wayne Dyer

You could be comparing yourself to a certain blogger, with no knowledge that that person has a whole team of people helping them to achieve the things they achieve. Or you might compare your photos to someone else's, without the knowledge that the specific blogger used to work as a photographer.

'Don't compare your beginning to someone else's middle' - Jon Acuff

So, you see you can't compare your story to someone else's, as you just don't have the full picture.

You might be nodding along realising that you're feeling those green-eyed monster vibes. If you are, let's focus on what to do to keep those feelings at bay.

First up, it's time to be really honest with yourself. What specifically is making you feel insecure? Do you feel you lack skills in a certain area? At this point I would spend time trying to get to the bottom of what it is that is causing you to doubt yourself, because you know it's about you, right?

Whatever you do in life and business, there will always people who are going to be doing it better than you, or, differently than you, and that's OK. You need to shift your focus from being concerned with other people, to focusing on yourself.

'Where the focus goes the energy flows. - Tony Robbins

You see you can't control what other people do, but you CAN control what you do and how you react. Set yourself your own goals and focus on these, not what other people are doing. Use that information as fuel, but not as a stick to beat yourself with.

Remember there's only one you.

'Today you are YOU, that is TRUER than true. There is NO ONE alive who is YOUER than YOU.' - Dr Seuss

You are unique and therefore so is your blog. If you show your personality through your content, there will be no other blog like it. Relish this, know your worth and NEVER forget it. Work hard to become the best version of yourself that you can be, showing this more and more to your audience every day and you will make your blog the best it can be.

By focusing on other people and what they're doing you are using up valuable time. You've probably moaned about the lack of time in a day available to you. Yet here you are wasting it by focusing in the wrong places. Believe me, there's so much that you could be doing to improve your own little piece of the internet. Obsessing over others is not productive. By spending less time worrying about other bloggers, you will have more time to put into your readers, your clients and yourself.

Time to develop a strategy

OK, I've spent lots of time so far telling you not to focus on other bloggers. However, knowing what other bloggers are doing can be important for research purposes, as we discussed earlier.

There's a major *BUT* coming. Don't be disheartened by their updates in your news feed. You can always unfollow people and clear up your news feed. You don't have to be bombarded by everyone's status updates constantly. Mute them or unfollow them and then when you want to do research go and look specifically at their channels. Otherwise we can end up spending too much time every day in *'consuming content'* mode. Which can cripple us and prevent us ever actually creating anything meaningful.

Often we are careful about what we put in our bodies, but we need to be as careful about what we allow into our minds.

There's an unlimited amount of space for bloggers. The internet won't suddenly become 'full'. As long as you're being authentic and working hard to give your readers the best content you can, another blogger cannot 'steal' your readers or your business.

'One can steal ideas. But no one can steal passion and execution.' - Tim Ferriss

You know what? Competition isn't always bad. It can actually be a good thing. Competition can push you to be more creative and to try new things. It can force you to get out of your comfort zone, to get uncomfortable. It's when we're uncomfortable that the magic often happens. Connecting with other bloggers is actually a fabulous way to form amazing online communities, which can benefit all involved.

Having friendships with people doing the same thing as you day in day out can be so powerful and everyone involved will be encouraged to raise their game and improve their individual blogs.

So, next time the green-eyed monster pays you a visit or when you feel unworthy, remember you cannot judge someone else's situation as you don't know what is going on behind the scenes. Turn these negative feelings into something positive. Work to improve the aspects of your own situation that will help you to feel more confident.

Bloggers don't get stuff 'for free'...

As you know, I started to blog to simply record our memories of our daughter, like an online, pimped-up baby book. Over the years, my blog has developed into so much more than that. A treasure chest of memories, a business and a place which helps other women learn the skills they need to succeed.

My blog is a space for me to be creatively free. I find it therapeutic to write things down and I also enjoy taking part in projects, the odd competition, and other opportunities. Over the years we've reviewed products, worked with many brands on sponsored content, been brand ambassadors and also been invited to cool events and sent on holiday.

All these things are wonderful and I'm very grateful. However, time and time again I've had people say, 'oh you got that for free' or 'you just had to write a post'. I even hear other bloggers saying things about 'freebies'.

Some people seem keen to start their own blog, as the 'stuff' they might get seems appealing. I encourage everyone who feels they want to blog to go ahead, jump in, the blogging community is so friendly and welcoming. Starting my blog is one of the best things I've ever done without a shadow of a doubt. One thing irks me though...

You see bloggers don't get stuff *for free*. Nope, not at all. They write conten, or make a video or use their social media platforms to promote the product in return for the product, an experience or a fee.

We spend time testing the products, spend time photographing them, editing the photos and pulling together a post. One which benefits the readers and shows the product in an accurate light. We spend a few hours on it one way or another AND we invest our skills. We then share the content with our audience; an audience we've spent months or even years growing and building relationships with.

So, DO people think blogging is an easy life? I LOVE blogging, I wish I had started sooner, but I think there's a massive misconception about the time bloggers put into their work. There's no doubt this varies massively from blogger to blogger, but I thought I'd just give a snapshot of my blogging week. For around three years I felt a pressure to post daily and if I posted a review I would also write another post too, just in case people weren't interested in reviews! Making a rod for my own back? Quite possibly, but I did it nevertheless.

Here's a summary of what my week used to look like

- I would spend most of my blogging time commenting on other blogger's content. There was a time when I first started blogging that I would comment on over 500 posts a week. I would also respond to blog comments, Facebook and Twitter ones and all comments on my Instagram images. That's A LOT of comments to write each week.

- I would post on my blog every day between one and four times. On average, I would be posting sixteen times a week. Therefore, I'd have to write fourteen posts and take half decent photos for the two posts a week that were photography based. Oh, and the stress when you got to the end of the week without a good shot, never mind... that's a whole other story.

- I'd also join in with projects, so I may have had to find time to do something, which I would then blog about. Maybe a DIY project, baking or even a day out.

- It would take around thirty minutes a day to schedule tweets, and other social media updates. I also had to link my posts to the relevant linkys each day, adding more time.

- Blogging is a social activity, so I would need to find time to interact with other bloggers, tweet and try to respond to everyone who tweets or retweets me.

- Then factor in time to brainstorm new ideas and ways of keeping things fresh.

- Devote time to building profiles and increasing followers on other social networks. Uploading photos to Instagram, pinning things and building boards in Pinterest.

- Looking for and responding to shout-outs for bloggers on Twitter and Facebook. Contacting PRs and dealing with emails from people who contacted me. There were, and still are, a LOT of daily emails to get through.

- I co-created #LittleFierceOnes on Instagram, which meant I had to find time to like all the pictures tagged and create a weekly post shouting out my favourites and reposting a picture each evening from the community.

Even now, over four years into my blog, every single child free second goes into blogging. If she's asleep in the car, I will be on my tablet blogging. When she's playing on her own for five minutes, I will be blogging. When I should be cooking, cleaning, washing, you've guessed it I will be blogging. I regularly stay up late working and I work every single night, without fail, often falling asleep at my laptop.

Do you think I got anything for 'free?'

So *please*, as a blogger, value yourself and value the effort and time you invest in building your blog. You get these opportunities to collaborate with brands because you've worked damn hard to build up your blog to that level.

Don't just accept any offer from a brand. Make sure it's right for you, your blog AND makes financial sense. If you're going to spend two hours creating a post and taking the necessary pictures, you need to make sure your time and skill is covered in the payment you receive. NOT just a fee equivalent to an hourly rate. Always remember to factor in all the hours you spent to get your blog to where it is today. It's those hours that are a vital component.

'The great time struggle' and the lies we tell ourselves...

Why do we waste our lives wishing we had more time? If I had more time I would have a tidy house. If I had more time I would exercise more. If I had more time I could plan better and lose weight. If I had more time, I would put more work into my blog. If I just had more time...

Sound familiar?

We don't make the most of our lives or our capabilities, as we are chasing something as mythical as a shiny winged unicorn. We put off so many things that could enrich our lives. Things that would make us happier and more successful. As we wait for a time in our lives when this '*more time*' will make itself known to us. We imagine it will come into our lives, bringing with it an ability for us to achieve and do all we want...

Only this will never happen as our priorities and our circumstances change. We fill our days with other 'important' stuff and we will still think the very same things we are thinking now. If only I had more time...

Here's the secret. We don't need more time.

Nope, not a single hour more.

What we need is more **focus.**

Modern life makes us think that we can have it all and do it all. While we can totally achieve what we desire, we can't do it all at the same time.

'We can do ANYTHING, just not EVERYTHING.' - David Allen

Society holds up multi-tasking as the goal which we should all be striving for. The skill that, if we nail it, our lives will be easier, and achievement will follow in spades.

Only it isn't, and it won't.

Multi-tasking splits our focus, meaning that while we can physically do more tasks, we do them all at a fraction of our ability. We lose time and focus forever transitioning between tasks and we spend far too much time on things that ultimately don't matter. —Like endlessly scrolling on Facebook looking for... Well, nothing —, there's no purpose to that is there?

We're actually handicapping ourselves when we try to multi-task. Even when we know for sure that focusing on one task means we perform better at that task. Picture trying to park the car in a tight spot. Your kids are fighting in the back of the car. What would you say? I'm guessing you would tell them to be quiet so you could concentrate on parking? Even though you could listen to them and park the car; your chances of not bumping the car in the next parking space is much higher if you're solely focused on driving (not refereeing!).

Although we acknowledge the need for a single-minded focus, when it comes down to it, in our daily personal and work lives we seem to imagine we'll be able to do all of our tasks at the same time. Checking Facebook while you're writing a blog post. Dipping in and out of our emails when we're trying to edit images or one of the hundreds of other tasks that seem to overwhelm us on a daily basis.

'If you really want to do something you'll a way. If you don't you'll find an excuse.' - Jim Rohn

I totally and wholeheartedly believe that the revered work-life balance is a myth and should not be held up at a goal for us all to strive for. To have a balance is to be average at both things you are trying to balance.

Being average doesn't tend itself to extraordinary results. Extraordinary performance requires people who are better than average. People who will put their heart, soul, passion, blood, sweat, and tears into their work. People who have a high degree of focus and give enough time to the projects that matter most.

'Magic happens at the extremes.' - Gary Keller

Achieving and being successful means there will be times when you feel out of balance. When you're focusing more on your work than the personal side of your life. Doing whatever it takes. This period of imbalance doesn't have to last forever, just long enough the make the difference. Then you can draw back and give other areas more attention.

To strive for the status quo is to strive for mediocrity.

We all have the same amount of time in a day. The thing that determines your success is what you do in this time and how big you think. If you think big you will achieve more in the same time than someone whose dreams are less ambitious.

So dare to dream big.

That's the secret. We don't need more time.

What we need is more **focus**.

'If you chase two rabbits, you will not catch either one' - Russian proverb

Sometimes our lack of focus can be due to too many opportunities, which is actually a great problem to have **IF** we know how to keep it in check and make it work for us.

Blogging can often be a case of feast or famine. Sometimes you're struggling for content inspiration, while other times you have so many ideas swirling around your head, that moving forward with any of them becomes difficult. I usually fall into the latter group. I find it hard to switch off, as I constantly have ideas popping into my head all competing for attention. Let me tell you it can be quite the party!

I'm not talking here about your daily to-do list, the posts you have committed to write or the projects you're being paid to work on. I'm talking about your ideas for things you want to write or change on your blog; your projects ideas and dreams.

Being a blogger is amazing. However, it does come with its own set of problems; long hours, lots of stress, and to-do lists that are often off the scale. Add in your family, pets, friends and the demands of daily life and it can be very easy to become overwhelmed. We've ALL been there, believe me.

As bloggers, we tend to do everything ourselves on our blogs, at least we do at the start. We can work on design, promotion, fixing issues, finances and everything else. Where do you start?

As we work for ourselves, we impose our own schedule and priorities. This is where overwhelm can start to creep in. We can, if we're not careful, become almost paralysed into inaction because we're analysing every aspect of what we should do, and consequently end up doing very little as a result.

I'm not immune to this and although I blog frequently about productivity, I still fall foul to overwhelm. There's always so much to do, so much to learn, so many possibilities. So much of EVERYTHING.

Commonly, what happens when we find ourselves overflowing with ideas, is that we do nothing, apart from maybe surf Facebook... We become paralysed from action by the fear of picking the wrong project or idea to progress with, which can be frustrating and is not very productive!

Although you haven't chosen your idea, your brain is trying to process all your ideas at once (to some degree). It's doing too much and splitting focus to the extent of inactivity.

I want to share how I move forward when overwhelm threatens to leave me hiding under the duvet! You can take these steps and use them in your own life to sharpen your focus and ditch overwhelm.

First things first. Do a time and motion study of how you spend your blogging time. How much time do you actually spend tab clicking, or scrolling through Facebook? Write it all down, then you can see where you are wasting your time and start to eliminate this time sucks from your day. Be meticulous and don't cheat. You're only lying to yourself.

Now this might sound too simplistic, but evaluate what you really have to get done each day. On the top of my list is content I've been paid to produce. Then things I have agreed to do for others. Followed by my own content, then the 'other' stuff at the bottom of the list.

The paid-for content is non-negotiable, as you have committed to producing that. Add in at the top of your list anything else that is non-negotiable. These non-negotiables aren't just things with a financial reward, but they are things that add value to your life in some way.

Feelings of overwhelm often means we can become a little unsettled. This means when we agree to do something, we can still be thinking about the other possibilities. Whether this is the right move for us, what else we have to do, and so on. Eliminate this by diving in fully and immersing yourself in the project.

Just because you have a fabulous idea, it doesn't mean you have to act on it immediately. We can all suffer from a degree of 'I-must-write-that-now-itis', but we CAN wait. Write down your idea, even set up a draft post, but you don't have to start working on it. Save it for when you have more time to commit to it fully.

Saying 'no' is also vital and is actually good for your business. I totally believe that not only is it empowering to say *no* to things which don't fit well with your blog, that aren't well paid enough or that simply don't light your fire. It can make PRs see you in a different light to those people blogging just for what they can get out of it.

When you're deciding which opportunities to accept, don't accept them all. Think about which align with your goals and those you will enjoy taking part in.

Remember, saying yes to things, means you are going to be taking time away from things you want to do; being with your kids, 'you time', time with family. Whatever it is, make sure it's worth it.

When overwhelm strikes fight back. Find your way of working it out. Whether that is brain dumping all of the things whizzing round your head and then making lists; whatever works for you. Use that innate fight or flight response to your benefit and fight!

Make sure you are giving the tasks you're working on 100% focus and use timers to help you. They will help to create a sense of motivation and urgency. When we work for ourselves, we don't have a boss giving us a deadline to get a project finished. This means we can often relax into our work. As a result, we may not be as productive as we would hope to be.

'The difference between a dream and a goal is a deadline' Gina Raimondo

By giving ourselves deadlines, we make sure that we are super productive in the time we have, without the need for a boss breathing down our necks!

Sometimes, if our overwhelm reoccurs, we may need to revisit what we are committing our time and resources to. Assess whether that's still beneficial to us at the current time. Do you need to take part in hundreds of linkys? Do you need to be as active in ALL your Facebook groups? Assess where you spend time and try to pinpoint what's overwhelming you. See if you still benefit from those activities and if not, simplify your life by ditching them.

Seth Godin was interviewed by Tim Ferriss about entrepreneurial block. Seth says, *"You get blocked, not because you're not passionate about what you're doing but because you are afraid."* Seth recommends that to conquer this, you need to do three things: 1) Be clear of what you are afraid of, 2) Know why you are afraid, 3) Commit to dancing with the fear because it will **never go away**.

If you're overwhelmed by video, but you know doing video would be really good for your business and would help you reach your audience more effectively. Then Seth would advise you to delve into what scares and makes you feel overwhelmed about the video and then do it! Just do it again and again, until eventually, overwhelm will disappear.

There are no quick fixes to sailing through life without a twinge of overwhelm. It takes effort and a regular reassessment of your goals and priorities. It's worth it though, to conquer overwhelm and know that you're on the way to achieving everything you want to.

There are certain productivity tactics that you can use to increase your working speed and output, especially batching and time blocking. Working in blocks will make the best use of your time. Batching gives you focus and eliminates the switching of setting up of tasks, leaving you to be more productive in less time.

If you really feel as if you NEED to post something on your blog, but you're struggling with writing time. Why not find an old post that's evergreen, give it a spring clean (maybe add a content upgrade) and republish it?

Why not ask a friend to write you a post for your blog or even rework an archived post from their blog? They will probably oblige; remember everyone loves a backlink! This will then give you time to focus on other aspects of your blog and clear some of the overwhelm as you do so.

Now we all love a list and lists are a great way to start to fight back against overwhelm. Aside from your daily to-do list you can create a list of all the projects you want to start and tasks you might like to do. Get them out of your mind on onto paper.

Then think about all the posts you might want to write and create another list. Getting all of these post ideas onto paper (or screen) just means less mental burden. Keeping everything in our heads is actually quite exhausting. So get it all out.

Next, think about your goals. If you're a visual person write these down too. Are you trying to increase your readership? Monetise more effectively? Collaborate with others? What do you want to near and long-term future to hold for your blog? Now go through your lists and see which project or idea fits with these goals. Every project you commit to and consequently give your time to, should be moving you forward towards your ultimate goals.

What's the 'why' for each of your ideas. Why do you want to do that particular project? Are you just jumping on a current trend? Is it to make money? What's the driving force behind each project idea? Make sure you are committing to projects that advance you towards your goals or that just make you happy. Avoid any that you are considering just because you feel you *should* do them.

This is where you can use your friends (even better if you have blogging friends) or family as sounding boards. Discuss your ideas and see which ones they think have more potential. Sometimes it's good to have fresh eyes on an idea to give another perspective.

Consider your time and resources, then be realistic. You might have some amazing ideas, but you don't have to implement them all right away. Maybe further down the road, you will have the time that a particular idea will need. Or maybe you need some resources that you don't have access to right now.

So, for these ideas, maybe now's not the right time for them to come to fruition. That's totally fine. It doesn't mean you're not going to work on them, just not now. Focus on what you have right now, the time and resources you have available to you at this present time and choose the projects that fit.

The other ideas needn't be forgotten about. Not at all, if they're good, then pop them onto a long-term content plan and revisit them in the future. Writing them down and allocating time to revisit them will mean you're more like to actually do that and make them work. Plus, they will not be taking up valuable headspace any longer.

So, write your lists, think about your goals, use your community. Assess the practicalities, but at the end move forward and take some action.

ABY'S ACTION STEP

Think about your current workload and commitments. Is there anything you're doing right now that no longer serves you? Anything you don't enjoy doing or that takes your valuable time and you can ditch without major repercussions? Just because you've always done something, doesn't mean you necessarily need to keep doing it.

CHAPTER 18

The struggle against our inner critics

I hope that as you read this book your life is on an even keel. I hope that you're not suffering from this overwhelm I've just spoken about. Or that you have feelings of inadequacy. Or a lack of confidence. That you're not super stressed about all the stuff going on in your life and feeling as if you're losing control. I hope this is not you… but I fear these words will be all too real for some of you.

We look at the online world, our peers, people we look up to, the people we think have 'made it' and it all seems so easy. They are so shiny with their perfect lives and we feel worse about ourselves. You might want what they have, for it to be *that* easy for you, but you never really know what goes on behind closed doors.

You see we are ALL fighting our own demons, whether they are related to our blogs or not, chances are these demons will affect them somehow. What I'm trying to

185

say is everyone is on their own journey and struggling with their own battles.

You might be feeling overwhelmed, but the best thing you can do is to get up and **keep going**. Whatever battle you're fighting; be that feeling of inadequacy or perhaps more serious mental health issues which threaten to kick your arse every day. **KEEP GOING.**

When the world deals you a, quite frankly, shit hand and you wonder how much more you can get through. **GET UP AND KEEP GOING**. Truly it's the only way to get through it and to come out the other side. You may be a bit battered and bruised, but you will definitely be more connected to those you love (there's always a silver lining).

We worry that we have so much to do, that we never get to the end of our to-do list and it makes us stressed. It starts to take over and threatens to take away our enjoyment for the thing we're meant to love. When you feel like this remember you are blessed to have the choices that lead to your overwhelm. Reframe it and you will see opportunity where you used to see overwhelm.
Those days when you think, 'seriously *this* as well?' When you wonder if someone up there is having a laugh at your expense; don't be a victim. Think day by day if you have to, hell hour by hour if it helps. Hold your family close and go into battle against the things that threaten to take you down. You are stronger than you think, you are braver than you know, and I know you CAN do this.

You WILL do this.

ABY'S ACTION STEP

Take ten minutes to sit with your eyes closed. Give yourself chance to focus on your successes and achievements. You will have done more than you give yourself credit for. Think about the things in your life that make you happy and the things that you are grateful for. If you're a parent, picture your child's face, that always brings me peace and helps me to put things into perspective.

Feeling the fear

I'd been blogging for around fifteen months when I was asked to speak out about my experience of post natal depression on the radio. At this point in my life, interviews and public speaking of any sort had always left me cold and totally petrified. Despite the huge amount of resistance I felt to saying yes; I agreed.

Three things made it impossible for me to say no. The first was that I'd promised myself at the start of 2015 I would feel the fear and do it anyway. To not let my worries prevent me from grabbing opportunities that may help me or possibly even others. The second reason, I was being asked to speak about post natal depression, which needs all the voices it can to raise awareness. To help women who are suffering feel less alone. The final reason was that Mumsnet had recommended me and I thought it was an honour to be given the chance to speak. So, I gave myself no choice.

My long-standing unease (OK petrifying fear) of public speaking, probably stemmed from a lack of confidence. In fact, for most of my life, I have activity avoided situations that would ask this of me. I decided no more; no longer would I be scared. Instead I would try to embrace these situations and see where they took me. Mumsnet were seeking mums with PND who hadn't sought help immediately. This was me, as I didn't go to my Doctor's for help until Ava was seven months old.

At the same time that I'd put my hat in the ring to talk on the radio, I was approached to do an interview with the Daily Mail. It would be focusing on a current story at the time which found that a third of all PND sufferers don't seek help from a medical professional. They're prevented from doing so by fears of being judged. Feeling as if they were letting their families down or over concerns they would be deemed an unfit mother; possibly running the risk of having their child taken away from them. Totally heart-breaking to feel like this.

They can't speak out, so I had to. I chatted with the journalist and the article ended up in the Daily Mail online. Some of the comments on the piece were shocking and showed what a long way we still have to go in terms of support and understanding around PND. It's an illness. Just like a broken leg, only you can't physically see the damage. It took me long enough to realise that.

Just as I was getting over being in a national paper (albeit online). It was time for the live radio interview. Alas it wasn't with my personal favourite, Grimmy. I was interviewed by the equally lovely Anne Diamond on BBC

Radio Berkshire. The words live... radio... interview would have previously had me running for the hills, but I'd played my 'feel the fear and do it anyway' mantra in my head a few times when I'd agreed.

I would like to say I felt like a pro, however, in reality I was petrified. Anne was really lovely though and apart from one moment, when I heard Ava shouting from downstairs (us Mamas got to do what we got to do!) which caused me to become a little distracted, I think I sounded OK. The main thing was, I DID IT! Following this, I also did another radio interview for a local station, Jack FM.

My first brush with the media and I can't think of a more important topic to speak about. There's so much ignorance and it's partly this ignorance that prevents many women from seeking the help they need.

The catalyst

I experienced a strange sense of power having overcome a fear as real as public speaking was to me. I felt propelled forward. I knew that I could achieve whatever I set my mind to. I didn't want to be stuck and held back by fear or worries. I just wanted to feel as if I had accomplished what I was capable of.

I'd had started to get really involved in the mechanics of blogging. How to create great posts and get them out in the world. At first, I thought, 'who am I to teach other bloggers how to do this stuff?' I was relatively new on the scene, but I had put the hours in. I may have just been blogging for a little while, but I had been consuming this information like it was a drug for months. I knew that I had information that could help others. I just had to be brave enough to share it and not worry about what anyone else thought.

Thankfully, I've only ever had great feedback, which continues to this day. This just goes to show that I needed to get out of my own way. People in my space knew me, they liked me, and they trusted what I had to say.

Developing the "know, like, and trust" factor

Let's get real here for a minute, people connect with and buy services and products from other people because they like them. Authenticity is so important in your business. In fact, it can sometimes be the most important aspect.

'People do not buy goods and services, they buy relations, stories, and magic.' - Seth Godin

OK so you realise the 'know, like and trust' factor is important, but how do you develop it with your audience?

Be the authentic you, embrace your quirks and don't apologise for it. Integrate the words that you say often in real life into your copy to show your readers the real you. Don't worry about turning someone off. Remember, if they don't like you, then they're not your perfect audience member anyway. You owe it to yourself and your true fans to be the *real* you. **Authenticity is key.**

It's so important in the blogging community to give more than you receive. It's a wonderful community and it really deserves to be looked after. As do the people in it. If you don't make money from your blog, you could give back by offering your advice, supporting people or helping their causes with your voice. If you do monetise, perhaps you can offer free content and products alongside your paid for goods and services. Keeping this balance shows people that you're a genuine person.

Make sure you are encouraging and relatable. Sharing your journey can be inspiring to your audience. You might encourage people to take a similar path to you and be able to help them along the way. However, you need to ensure that you share the difficulties too. To show them the 'less-than-perfect' real parts as well. Otherwise, you may come across as unattainable and the chances of developing the KLT factor will diminish.

Let's go one step further

Let's break it down and look at ways you can give your audience chance to get to *know* you. Writing great quality posts is obviously key. These will position you as an expert and confirm your authority in your niche, so more people will be aware of you. If you know who your ideal reader is, you will be able to write content that answers their needs. This is vital to being able to develop the relationship with them. You need to know who you're speaking to.

When you know this, you are able to research what your audience needs. Then create content that helps them and alleviates their particular pain points. Speaking to their core desires and providing content that moves them forward is crucial.

When you write a post, try to add in a free digital download of some sort which ties into the post and would be useful to your audience. This opt-in freebie helps your audience AND helps you to build your email list, which will further help you develop this 'know' factor. A relationship with a key influencer can really help you develop your perceived authority. You will gain immediate authority by association.

You can use social networking and blog post commenting to start a relationship with key influencers in your niche. Create great and useful content so people feel compelled to share it, meaning you will reach a whole new audience. The more you're seen talking about your topic, the more people will start to associate you with the expert in that niche.

Focus on producing posts which are filled with fab content and that show your personality. Guest posting on other sites is also a great way to build these 'know' connections with other people's audience.

Now people *know* you, they have to *like* you too! If you were personally interested in purchasing a product, for example, maybe an hour of coaching. Would you buy it from someone you liked or someone you felt ambivalent about? Yes, you'd buy from the one you liked. People connect with people and showing your face on your site gives your audience chance to 'like' you and connect with you. When they're reading your blog, having this picture of you helps them know who's talking to them and makes the experience feel more complete.

This shouldn't really have to be said, but I will say it anyway. Be a nice person in all your online interactions. Show your vulnerability and show that you're a human. This will help people connect with you and probably like you too. Using video and platforms such a Facebook Lives can be really useful too. They really help people see what you're like (in real life) and develop the connection with you. Personally, I love Facebook Live and feel it has helped me create a stronger bond with my community.

If you're creating content that will help your readers to solve their issues. They will then love you for it. Always go above and beyond with the free content you offer.

Use any opportunity you have to start a conversation with your audience. Ask them for feedback and then make sure you respond to them when they offer it!

The trust element is a really important factor when you begin selling online. Always deliver, over deliver and try to amaze people with the content you have produced.

Make people think, 'wow, if she's given this for free, just imagine what her paid products are like'.

Your audience needs to know the level of quality to expect if they buy a product from you. They will lose confidence if the quality of your work varies.

This goes back to social proof, but people gain confidence in the positive experience of others. So, including testimonials on your sales page would be a great idea. Offering a money back guarantee will also give people more confidence to buy, by lowering the perceived risk.

However, you're never going to get a chance to develop this know, like and trust factor if you're hiding away, too scared to step up and actually be heard.

Self-promotion can seem a bit icky. It can jar with us and make us feel as if others will judge us negatively; thinking we're *up ourselves*. The thing is if you don't step out of the shadows you won't achieve what you want in life. You need **visibility**. Someone somewhere needs your message, they need **YOU**.

So you have to get visible.

CHAPTER 19

How to overcome the fear of self-promotion

Firstly, let me back-track, I'm not suggesting that we lose all sense of social awareness and turn into those people who won't stop talking about themselves. We *ALL* know people like that, don't we?!

However, you need to be your own cheerleader, promoting yourself and your blog when and where appropriate.

Often our blogs are personal, and I think that's where the difficulty lies for many of us. We need to remember it's business and self-promotion is so important to help you get your blog out there and vital to the success of your blog.

Many people struggle to know how to promote themselves and how to do it without feeling 'icky'.

How do you pull this off without feeling like a bragger?

Confidence in your ability is key. If you aren't confident about your content, it follows that you won't be confident about promoting it or promoting yourself. Drilling down who your target audience is means you will be able to create content specifically for them. In turn, you'll be more confident that you're producing great content that your audience needs.

We are often our own worst critics. When that nagging voice appears on your shoulder saying you're not good enough, make sure you smack it off by countering it with something you like (or appreciate) about yourself. You are JUST as good as everyone else. Don't let these nagging voices win. Also remember, don't compare your beginning to someone else's middle. That's a sure-fire way to feel rubbish.

What scares you the most? Are you worried about what others will think? Of being rejected? Do you feel more vulnerable when you share your work? To get rid of these fears you have to know specifically what they are and where they stem from.

Developing a better relationship with yourself is really important. This won't happen overnight but start to be more compassionate towards your own flaws. Treat yourself to the same levels of compassion that you would give others. Most of us need to give ourselves a break!

How do you feel when someone gives you a compliment? You might feel happier, maybe even a bit more confident? We shouldn't have to rely on others to give us this validation and make us feel better. We need to do it for ourselves by being realistic, but positive.

Promoting your content can feel like a hard sell, especially if you have a virtual product to sell such as an e-book or a course. Just remember *why* you wrote the e-book or *why* you wrote that last blog post. It was to help people; to give them the information they want or need. So, by reaching out to them, you're in fact helping them find good information to help them solve their current need.

Don't expect miracles; but do remind yourself that there are people out there who need what you have to offer. Your job is to let them know where the content is that can help them.

ABY'S ACTION STEP

Write down seven promotional activities that make you feel apprehensive and do one each day for the next week. This could be writing a guest post, getting a collaboration going, sharing posts more thoroughly on social media, for example.

How to sum up what you do in a nutshell

Now, imagine you're at an event and your dream brand asks you about your blog. If you can't quickly summarise what your blog is all about, it will be hard to feel confident. Stumbling over your words will make any confidence you do have quickly evaporate. You need to have an elevator pitch. An elevator pitch is a short summary of what your business is and who (and how) it helps your ideal audience.

I tend to follow this structure, 'I help [your idea audience] to [whatever their goal is] by [how you help them] so that they [the core desire of your ideal audience member]. Want a peek at mine? 'I help mum bloggers to turn their blog into a business by providing them with a structured roadmap, courses and coaching so that they can work from home and have more freedom in their lives.'

Now, write yours and then learn it off by heart. Memorise it until it trips off your tongue without you even having to think.

Learn from the people who are confident with marketing themselves. Enjoy being in the presence of these amazing people and start believing that you're one of them, rather than feeling that you don't belong in their company. Remember, research has shown you are the sum of the five people you spend the most time with, so spend time with people who have what you want. This could be in terms of characteristics or success.

ABY'S ACTION STEP

Write your elevator pitch.

I help [your idea audience] to [whatever their goal is] by [how you help them] so that they [the core desire of your ideal audience member].

Believe in yourself and your blog

'What if I fly' - Erin Hanson

I've spoken already about how our minds are a powerful tool and while they can negatively impact on our lives, they can also have such a positive effect too.

If we work hard and believe in ourselves, we can do great things. If you're not confident about your content, whether that's vlogs, podcasts, posts or e-books, no-one else is going to feel confident in you. You're producing great content, **you are worthy** of the success you want, **believe** it and **show people**.

Sometimes when we start believing in ourselves the universe sends us wonderful opportunities...

An extraordinary press trip with Bridgestone - January 2016

A few weeks before Christmas 2015, I was invited on a press trip to the French Riveria by Bridgestone Tyres. I'd been lucky to travel to Rome with them in 2015 and doubly blessed to then receive this invitation.

In life, we have moments that we will always remember. They might have seemed insignificant in the moment, but sometimes they are more impactful than we realised at the time.

It was the start of the journey and I was sitting on the plane looking around at the other people who were on the press trip. The plane was full of journalists working for major national papers. Journalists whose bosses and titles had put them on that plane; en-route to what would transpire to be an amazing experience. I remember stopping in my tracks and thinking, I'd put *myself* on that plane.

I'd got there by building up my blog, developing relationships with brands and by making sure I did a great job with all the brands I worked with. As I took in that amazing experience, I was so thankful for my blog. Thankful also for the persistence and drive I had in me, which had allowed my blog grow and put me there.

I rarely allow myself a proud moment, but I allowed myself that one.

After the flight and a coach trip, we arrived in Monaco at the Fairmont Hotel. Positioned on the hairpin bend on the Grand Prix circuit, this beautiful hotel had stunning sea views to the rear. It was totally breath-taking. We wandered along the seafront and took in all the sights. We reached the Champions Promenade, which features the footprints of so many famous footballers, and slipped off our shoes to stand in their imprints. Listening to the sea lap on the shore, mesmerised by the twinkly lights from the bars and restaurants all around.

During the evening we headed to the legendary Monte-Carlo Casino. An incredible building with stunning architecture similar to that of a palace, it was amazing. After a few 'small' bets we retired to the hotel bar (which was within Nobo) and chatted until the early hours with the other writers and the Bridgestone team. It was quite late when we eventually hit the hay... The next day we were up and out of the hotel early to head to a Chateaux for the product unveiling. We spent most of the day driving cars round the twisty mountain roads, taking in the views and eating scrummy food. Before heading to our new hotel, the Grand Hyatt Martinez in Cannes located on the prestigious Boulevard de la Croisette.

I felt as if I was starring in the Great Gatsby. The Martinez is such an imposingly elegant art deco hotel. Set on the Cannes seafront, it was like stepping back to the roaring 20s. After a little local exploration, we decided to get ready and head to the hotel bar for a cheeky cocktail. We enjoyed another wonderful night in a local restaurant, where we laughed until our sides hurt. Everyone on the trip bonded so well, which made for a good crack and a truly memorable experience.

The following day was a day of fun, starting with driving classic sports cars. Outside the hotel waiting for us was five million pounds worth of classic cars. These cars had been the stars of many shows and films over the years. As you can imagine it was quite an amazing sight! I hopped in the back of the DB9 (of James Bond fame) with a friend and were driven by two chaps on our trip. Driving along the Cannes seafront in a DB9 with the sun beating down on us is not what I usually expect from a January day.

With the wind in my hair, we continued to speed down the seafront. The winter sun making it a perfect moment to catch myself and realise that this was actually happening to me. I had to pinch myself to ensure it wasn't a dream. I was very proud that my blog had got me there.

Although the sun was shining, we ended up sitting with a blanket over us; we must have looked like Driving Miss Daisy! As we drove round Cannes in a twenty-thirty car convoy it was so hard to capture all the wonderful sights on my trusty camera, but I will remember it forever.

We ventured to a lighthouse and swapped cars, so we got to experience another awesome classic car. This time I hitched a ride in a Ford Mustang, which was much more comfortable than the DB9. The back of that sports car was not designed for long legs and I had the bruises to prove it!

The next part of our day was Macaron making at the Majestic Barriere, another prestigious hotel a little further along the promenade than the Martinez. Soon lunch was calling. I'd never expected such a magnificent venue in which to dine. We walked down the steps, almost as if we were just going to the beach and then we saw the stunning restaurant, with full glass sliding doors opening right out onto the glorious sandy beach.

As we had come to expect on our trip, the food was delightful. We were well and truly spoiled by Bridgestone, yet again. We took one last look at the classic cars on the walk back to the hotel. We then had a few hours to kill before leaving for the airport, so I enjoyed a much-appreciated massage, compliments of Bridgestone. It was a truly unforgettable experience.

CHAPTER 20

My biggest blogging regret.

In the interest of balance and after sharing one of my highlights with you, I want to share my biggest regret. I don't want you to think my journey has been easy and that I didn't make any mistakes. Good lord, I've made loads! One of my biggest was not really learning about SEO (Search Engine Optimisation) early enough. Then, even when I did know the importance of SEO I was publishing too much content every day to have time to actually implement what I knew. BIG mistake! HUGE!

SEO is not sexy, it's not even very interesting to most people unless you're Rand Fishkin from Moz. It can be a dry topic, BUT it *really* works and gives you the best chance of visibility, when combined with other marketing strategy.

The SEO of your site can be improved in numerous different ways and there are multiple factors which contribute to how well your site does in search. I want to share with you some things you can start doing right now to begin to improve your site's SEO.

Start guest posting on high-ranking sites. By doing this you will get a precious backlink, which boosts your site's SEO. Not only that, but the backlink will have more authority than those from lower ranked sites; Google will like that.

Using long tail keywords will also really help you. Over 70% of google search terms are long tail keywords. Long-tail keywords are made up of three or more words. They are more specific and bring more targeted visitors to your blog.

Think about posting about your beach holiday in Spain. Imagine how many websites have used the keywords 'Spain'. Wait I'll tell you... 358 million! Yep, that's right, so your blog post will be number 350,000,001. However, if you use 'gluten-free beach holiday in Spain with a toddler' (for example), it drops to 1,210,000. There are fewer people searching for that specific term, but your post will be MUCH more visible to the people wanting to read EXACTLY your content. More people will read your post and Google will decide you're an authority and a trusted site. Therefore, they will rank you higher.

Coding around your text highlights to the search bots the important parts of your post. Use formatting such as <H3> headings. Making sure you have a unique and relevant title for each page. Also, that all of your pages have a proper meta tag descriptions.

Blog speed is a big issue and one which is often overlooked. The faster your blog loads, the happier your readers will be. They will return more often and Google will notice this. There are various ways to speed up your blog and reducing the size of the images you add before you upload them can be a great help.

As social media is contributing more to SEO all the time, make sure you are using the keywords from your posts on social too.

Have you submitted a sitemap to search engines? Sitemaps are really just a map of the content on your site and will help your content be found on search. This might seem very complicated, however, there's a WordPress plugin called the Google XML Sitemap Generator or you can use Yoast.

Most bloggers I know don't share their content enough. It's so important to promote your content and part of this is making sure that people can share your posts easily. This might seem a bit obvious, but the easier it is to share your posts, the more people will do so and consequently the more traffic you will get. It will please Google in the process too.

Although it seems to have fallen out of favour for many bloggers, sharing your post on Google+ will help your SEO more than a share on any other social media platform (assuming your follower numbers are equal).

Do you email your posts to your email list? Remember one of the highest factors in terms of influence on the search engine rankings is still traffic. The more traffic you can drive to your post the more this will boost your SEO and your rankings.

Search traffic has intent, they have typed something into Google that they want the answer to. As opposed to social media traffic, which has way less intent and is more opportunistic. They want your content more because they are actively looking for it, rather than just happened to see a tweet to a post you shared on Twitter.

There's no doubt that if you get SEO keyword research right it's one of the only FREE ways to build your blog and increase traffic. As the subject is a little dry (alright downright boring!), it can be easy to gloss over it and go looking for something more exciting to do with our time. We really shouldn't, as getting it right is so important. Not having an SEO strategy right from the start is one of my main blogging regrets.

So how do you get it right? Well it all starts with keyword research

Without keyword research, you could be using keywords that people aren't looking for or keywords that are hugely competitive and that you would struggle to even be seen in the search results. Which does not help your organic traffic growth... Don't use words that simply describe your content. You need to use the words your ideal audience is using to try and find content like yours.

Keyword research tells you what these words are, so you don't need to guess. It's all there for you. When you've found these perfect keywords you can optimise your post to include them. Meaning your ideal audience will begin to find your content in response to their searches.

You will need to find the best keywords for the pages on your site and then make sure for each post you write you are picking specific keywords.

Before you start creating your next blog post, it's time to do your research. There's no point in writing the post then having to rewrite chunks to squeeze in your keywords. You want to use your keywords in a natural way and so it's much easier to know what your keywords are before you start.

How to do SEO keyword research

You will need to get yourself a free Google AdWords account. Signing up for a free account will give you access to the Keyword tool. There are other keyword tools, just running a Google search will give you other options to try if you prefer.

Each tool will have a slightly different way of working. However, in general you pop in your keyword idea and then the tool will suggest similar keywords that people are actually searching for. Then you can evaluate which of your keyword ideas is the best for your post.

In other words, which one has the most people searching for it. Ideally, you want a high search volume BUT low to medium competition. Trying to rank for keyword phrases with high competition might not be the best idea.

You will have to use your judgement whether the potential search volume for a term is enough to make it worthwhile optimising for that particular keyword. If only thirty people are searching, you might want to pick something else. If you find something with a decent number of searches, low-medium competition AND a keyword phrase you feel you could naturally weave into your posts then you have your keyword.

Now you have your keywords, you need to make sure you are using them for maximum impact. With your keyword or keyword phrase in mind, just write your post. If there's a way when writing this first draft to use your keyword in the copy then do so, but don't worry too much about getting it all perfect straight away. That's what editing is for!

When you've created your masterpiece you need to focus on these factors. How often the keyword appears in the post (keyword density), the variations of the main keyword (keyword variations or related keywords) and where they appear in the post (keyword location).

Your keywords should take up at least 1.5% of the total word count. Mentioning it once will not cut it! The fact that keywords variations still help your SEO means that we can all avoid writing like a robot, trying to squeeze in the exact keyword phrase multiple times. Often it will sound more natural to use a variation in certain places of your copy, to help it flow better.

I'm sure you know by now that you're meant to use your SEO keyword phrase numerous times throughout your post, which is true. However, you need to make sure you use your keyword in certain key locations. Your post URL. In the title of your post ideally at the start, within the first 100 words of text and in at least one heading (H2, H3 etc.)

When you're editing the post, are there occasions when you could have used the keyword phrase or a variation? If so, put them in. Change up the headers to make sure the keyword phrase is in some of them. The focus on the first hundred words and double check that your keyword phrase is there.

Make sure your introduction is going to hook the reader into wanting to read on. Can you add any related keywords in at this stage? This will help signal to Google what the content is about and it will help the overall post SEO.

Make sure that you don't become too SEO keyword focused at the expense of the quality of your content. People want to read real people's words and so keep the 'you' in your posts.

As well as for each post, you need to pick keywords for your pages. These are *seed keywords*. Seed keywords are foundation keywords for SEO.

The meaning of these keywords is not changed by modifier words. So, for example, if you had a weight loss blog. Your seed keyword might be *'weight loss'*. The long tail keywords are the seed keywords + modifier. For example; *weight loss pills, weight loss classes, weight loss for the over 50s*. With *weight loss* being the seed and the other words the modifiers.

ABY'S ACTION STEP

Brainstorm ten seed keywords for your site. Think about what you do and what do you want to be found for?

Let's now look at SEO page titles and descriptions. These tell Google what your blog is about so they can suggest your content in the relevant search results for the right people.

This information is also called SEO meta data and you really need to get this stuff right, if you want to increase your search rankings and grow your blog traffic.

For clarity, your posts SEO page title is the text that appears in the Google search result and at the top of your browser window. The posts SEO page description is the text explaining what the post or page is about in the Google search result.

We need to tell Google what your site and posts are about by optimising your posts and pages properly. As you've probably guessed SEO page titles and descriptions should be just one part of your overall SEO strategy. For example, if you fully optimise your posts, but your site takes twenty minutes to load and is full of broken links, then you won't see the benefits of the on-page SEO.

If you're new to SEO, then start by optimising your posts. You can then build up and improve the other aspects as you move forward. Learning how to write SEO page titles and descriptions is super important to ensure Google has the best possible information.

Writing your post title isn't about plucking something relevant out of thin air and hoping for the best. You need to make sure the title you choose accurately represents your content AND includes your keywords.

I use the Yoast SEO WordPress plugin to help make sure my on-page SEO is good for each post and page I write. If you haven't already you might want to check out the free Yoast version. SEO page titles need to be kept under sixty characters. Otherwise, the end will be cut off in the search results. Including your keywords at the beginning will improve the SEO, although bear in mind reader experience too.

If you want to check how good your headline is, you can check out the CoSchedule headline tool, which grades headlines on multiple factors. You might find making one small tweak helps to improve your headline.

When writing your **meta data** it's important not to stuff the description with your keyword. Placing it once, near to the beginning is fine. Think also about what would make you click? It needs to accurately tell the potential reader what the post/page is about and how they will benefit from reading.

Need an example? Say my main keyword phrase is "become a brand ambassador". The **SEO page title** is: How to become a brand ambassador. The **meta data** could be: "Become a Brand Ambassador to really improve your blog income and your exposure. Learn how to find and secure these lucrative contracts."

Using Yoast makes all the SEO optimising super simple. You just pop in your target keyword, page title, and page meta description into the Yoast panel which will appear on your WordPress post when you install the plugin. Then, Yoast will analyse your post and show you via a handy traffic light system whether the content optimised well or not.

SEO is obviously way more complicated and intricate than just using Yoast and finding the right keywords for your posts. Although it might not be everyone's favourite topic, there's so much we can receive in terms of results from investing a little effort.

How else can you improve your SEO? Let's start at the beginning. Have you verified your blog with the Google Search Console? *silence*. OK then, I'll take that as a *no*. For those who have, hang on one minute and I'll be back with you....

For those of you who have no idea what I'm talking about, you need to verify your blog with the Google Search Console. This keeps track of your site and gives

Google information about your site's identity, changes and updates. It also controls how your site appears in search results. First step, pop on over and set up a free account. Log in with a Google account (@gmail.com email or G Suite account email).

Then enter your website URL in the box and add a property. You'll want to add four different variations of your URL, like this:

https://youbabememummy.com
https://www.youbabememummy.com.
http://youbabememummy.com
http://www.youbabememummy.com

Create a set and add all four properties to the set. By doing this you're telling Google that, no matter which URL variation comes up in search results, they are all the same website.

You'll then see various verification methods. The easiest one is to verify with Google Analytics, which you can find on the Alternate Methods tab. If your Google Analytics account is setup with the same gmail.com address your site will verify immediately. Otherwise, you can download an HTML file and upload it to your site to complete verification.

Head to the crawl tab, as that's the one related to SEO. Check how often Google crawls your blog. Click on Crawl Stats and you will see graphs which represents when the Google search algorithm is scanning your site looking for changes. The more crawls it's doing the better, as it means it is going to always have the most up-to-date version of your blog. Don't go crazy though as it might put pressure on your server if you crank it up too much.

Now check your sitemap. Click sitemaps (also in the Crawl section) and check to see if there's a sitemap already submitted. If not, you can add one manually. Just remove outdated or invalid sitemaps like sitemap.xml and click the Add/Test Sitemap button in the top right. Then enter sitemap_index.xml into the text box that appears and press Submit.

Keeping your post URLs clean will also benefit you in terms of SEO juice. Ideally, avoid having the dates from in your post URLs as this dates content quickly. Also having a super long URL makes it harder for Google to index. You can customise your post URL before you publish to ensure its SEO optimised (short and keywords included).

Do your best to select the right keyword and then to use it well within your post. Never stuff your post with keywords or change your tone to suit the SEO.

It's also so important remember to interlink your posts to create a solid internal link structure. This helps keep people on your site longer, lowers your bounce rate, and gives you longer to develop the know, like and trust factor. It's so easy to do and if you have Yoast Premium, it even suggests links you might like to add to each post from the content on your site.

By interlinking, all you're doing is suggesting another blog post of yours to your readers. Don't overdo it, but interlinking posts creates a great site structure that the search bots will love. Make sure you do this linking on older posts too (add in links to more current posts). It's easier to link to older posts when we are writing fresh content, but we sometimes fail to go back and add links to those older ones too. So, make sure you think about those old posts too.

Remember your content shouldn't just have one life. It can have so many lives if we're clever. It's good practice to keep your archived content up to date as this helps your blog's SEO and provides a better-quality experience for your reader.

Also, when you make a change to a post, ask Google to re-crawl your site to index those recent changes. Which means your position in the search engine results could improve quicker, than if we wait for Google to recrawl on their schedule.

When you update an older post, pay particular attention to the content, is anything outdated? Could you update it in some way? Are the images good (I cringe at some of my early ones!)? Could you do better in terms of optimising for SEO? Lastly, double check your internal and external links and you should be good to go.

CHAPTER 21

Shall I share another regret?

Alongside the woeful lack of SEO in my early posts, I also really regret not realising the power of having my own email list of subscribers. As I mentioned, when I started blogging, I didn't see anyone talking about lists. Consequently, while I was consuming all the content I possibly could, email lists passed me by.

Do you have an email list for your blog? Maybe you haven't got one, but feel as if you should? Perhaps you aren't even sure why you should have one, but everyone else seems to be doing it.

With so many blogging tasks demanding your time, it can be a little daunting to take on yet another regular task. I want to tell you why creating an email list and focusing on building this is a good use of your time.

You have complete control over it

You control what you decide to publish on your blog and you also control the social media content you send out into the world. What you can't control, however, is the networks you send your content out on.

You don't own Instagram or Facebook (although that would be nice!). You use these networks to drive traffic to your blog, but what if Facebook shuts up shop? You've spent years building up a page, which drives significant traffic to your blog and just like that it's gone. Unlikely, but you don't own Facebook, so you have no control over it. The same could be possible for any social network. Algorithms change and who knows how our content will be shared by these networks in the future.

Would you build a house on rented land?

The good news is you can control your email list. So, regardless of what Instagram gets up to in the future or how few people Facebook decides to show your updates to, you will have built a list of invested followers, who are waiting to read your content.

You're in the inner circle AKA their personal inbox

Most people use their emails quite a lot and if you're anything like me, your email is pretty much open all day. Email is a quick, easy and direct method of making sure your message reaches your audience.

Most of the time the messages that people have in their inboxes are about things they care about and that's a lovely position to be in. On social media platforms, your message is one of many others by other brands and blogs. So, even if someone is interested in your blog, the chances of them seeing your message is small. They have much more chance of seeing your email.

A good relationship with your audience is a very important factor in the growth and success of your blog. People want to feel as if they're part of your journey. Reaching a person's inbox is a wonderful way to be able to do this and to help to build strong relationships. If you offer exclusive content of some form, they will feel special and valued (as they should be being in your tribe). Your audience will also trust you more, as you will become a regular fixture in their lives.

Your email list is also a very cost-effective form of marketing. I used to sell print advertising and believe me that stuff isn't cheap! It also has a limited shelf life in most cases. Email gets your message out in a really cheap way. Most email providers have free options for smaller email lists and you can upgrade as your list grows. Still so much cheaper than a newspaper ad!

Your email marketing software will give you a great deal of information in relation to analytics. You'll know which of your campaigns gets the most clicks and which email titles leads to a better open rate. This information will help you tailor your correspondence to make sure you are giving your audience what they want, which will encourage them to stay on your list.

When you think about the future of your blog, do you think you will ever have a product to sell? An e-book, a course or even some lovely printables. If you think this is a possibility (and it should be), then you definitely need a list, like yesterday. Even if this idea is so far in the future you haven't really thought about it, start building your list now. Maybe you never want your own products, you still need a list because you shouldn't build your business on rented land.

If someone is subscribing to your blog, they love what you do, believe me, I follow far more people on social media than the number I subscribe to. Why is this relevant? I'm SO MUCH more likely to buy something from a blog I subscribe to than from one I just follow. Even if you aren't planning a 'product' to sell, don't forget about affiliate marketing. The recommendations you make in your email marketing can also earn you money.

Email is also such an easy and quick way to share information and you can be *more* confident that people are going to see your message. As discussed, they may not see your Facebook update or notice your tweet, but they probably at least saw your email. Hopefully, they opened it too!

I do like to get on my soap box about the fact that all bloggers need an email list. My email list is so important to my blog. It allows me to create a better connection with my readers and develop more meaningful relationships.

What you'll need before you start to grow your email list

You're going to be collecting lots of email addresses, so you need a great list building software. This will allow you to store them, organise them and make it super easy to communicate with your followers.

I use Convertkit, as it's made specifically for bloggers by bloggers. It has such great functionality and is easy to use. However, if you want to start for free, MailChimp has a free option, which could be a good place to start. Set yourself up with an account and let's get started!

Your blog content needs to be part of a larger strategy. A well-thought-out plan, driving towards a certain end-goal. Creating epic blog posts helps you create a solid base of content for your blog, increases traffic, grows awareness of your blog and creates awesome foundations for your blog biz.

Blog content gives you an opportunity to teach, entertain, inform, and make connections with your audience. It gives people an opportunity to try before they buy. They can make sure they get value from your content before they hand over their email to you.

Solid blog content also helps you to build authority and credibility within your niche, you will start to be known for having those specific skills or that specific knowledge.

Let's chat about how you can create a list-building blog post.

Occasionally, you might want to write purely for pleasure and share something on your blog that isn't particularly relevant to your goals. However, if you want to monetise your blog and build your list, the majority of your content needs to be well thought out and the sort of content that your ideal reader actually wants to read. Content that solves their problem or answers their current need.

As I mentioned earlier you need to find out what problems your ideal audience has and then create content that solves these problems. Simples! What questions to your ideal readers ask? Whether they have asked the question to you directly. Or asked it in a Facebook group or when responding to your emails.

These questions can help you formulate a content plan that meets their needs. Keep a note somewhere of these questions as they come up. This will build into an invaluable inspiration swipe file that you can refer to as you're creating future content.

Make sure you have picked the right keywords and then get to work creating your post outline. Think about the opening, the hook, the meat of the post, the conclusion and finally the call to action. Aim to take your readers on a journey from where they are now to where they want to be through your post.

Divide up the post using bullet points, headers (which you now know are good for SEO), bold text, images and possibly, other sorts of media.

For these epic list-building posts aim for longer form content. Google favours long-form content, so 1,500-2,000 is a good word count to aim for. The most shared posts on social media are on average 2.2k words in length. These words do have to be valuable content though, there's no benefit to adding fluff in order to bulk up the post. As I mentioned above your content should solve a problem. It should get your reader from point A to point B (point B being they are more informed, entertained or their problem has been solved).

Keep the information actionable. Share the 'what', 'why' and 'how'. Outline their problem, why they have it and how they solve it, step by step. Add some screenshots or maybe a quick video if it will help make your point. Think about how you can best share the information in your post.

Make sure you have used your keyword phrase, labelled your images to include your keyword phrase and that you have a great pin on the post with a descriptive description including your keywords. Add the keywords to the alt text of the picture and to relevant headers (H2, H3 etc), make sure it's in your opening paragraph and the post URL and you should be almost there.

You obviously want to create content to get traffic, but you also need that traffic to be reoccurring. Otherwise, you will have to continually get new people all over again each month. A great way to encourage repeat visitors by developing a connection with them and a great way to develop a connection is by getting them on your email list. You can do this by offering them a freebie piece of content in return for their email address (opt-in freebie/content upgrade/lead magnet).

Once you've written this epic post, think what would be really helpful for the reader now. If it's a recipe, then perhaps it would be useful to have a meal planner or a shopping list. Just think of the next step and create something to help with that. Think about keeping it short and with the aim of giving the reader a quick win.

Take some time to create the copy on the opt-in forms. It's really important to pick your copy carefully on these forms to make it as attractive as possible. No-one wants to 'subscribe'. They certainly don't want to do it just so they 'never miss a post'. It's just not compelling enough. You need to offer them something helpful, desirable; something that is worth trading their email address for. The language you use should be more dynamic and emotive.

Now, you have your awesome actionable, SEO optimised blog post complete with opt-in freebie. You need to promote that sucker. Don't just send one tweet and be done. Nope, my friend. That is not enough. That post needs to go out once or twice on Facebook and have recurring tweets driving people back to the post. You can then pin one of those tweets, so it stays right at the top of your feed. Then share on Instagram, mention it on Instagram stories or on a Facebook Live. Keep getting the word out about this awesome piece of content. This will then drive more traffic to the post and help you grow your email list.

This foundational post will then act as pillar content on your blog and, as long as it's evergreen in nature, can continue to drive traffic for years to come. Building your authority and also driving email sign-ups for years to come too!

I love using Snip.ly to add a link and call to action to any link you share (from a third party). Programmes like these make it possible to add your opt-in to someone else's site via a specially created link. Super clever!

Make sure you update your email signature and pop your opt-in freebie in there, to make the most of all those emails you send. I always have one of my free challenges in my signature.

You can also create an out of office response which you leave on all the time. In this email you would state things relevant to your particular business and let people know you will respond within a certain timescale. You could also highlight your freebie in here too!

One of the best ways I have found to grow my list is by running a free challenge. I've done quite a few over the years and people LOVE a challenge. It's also a wonderful way to demonstrate how you work and show your experience. You're also giving your audience a chance to develop a connection with you.

You might even want to consider adding a link to your opt-in to your menu. This is a great way to highlight your freebie. This way it will be prominent and hopefully the positioning will lead to more clicks and sign-ups.

Utilising a welcome mat isn't an option for everyone. However, the stats prove that they do work. A welcome mat covers the homepage when someone arrives on your site. The reader can then either opt-in or close out of the landing page to see your site. If the offer is good enough they tend to work really well. Although, it's more of an aggressive marketing tactic than some of the other options.

My preference is an exit intent pop up. This is such a clever piece of technology. It lies dormant until someone moves their mouse up to the X to close the page, then it springs into action to share a must-have freebie.

If you're a forum user, then update your forum signature with a link to your opt in landing page. Post your blog posts to medium.com and include your opt-in's there too. Or simply share you opt in on Reddit within the rules of the site of course!

I've touched on guest posting being a great way to widen your audience, but many people waste the opportunity. The hosts audience might read your guest post. They may even pop to your site, but after that, they'll probably forget about you.

However, if you create an awesome content upgrade specifically for your guest post, then those people will opt in to your list. Then you have a chance to develop a relationship with them. You can do the same as a guest on podcasts too. So, if you can get on one, it can be good for your exposure. As with guest posting, create a custom, relevant download and offer it to the listeners.

You might already have a few freebies on your blog already. If this sounds like you, then you should consider creating a resource library. These are a way to give lots of value to your readers. You might be thinking, well they can already get all of those freebies from my blog already, but what a resource library does is it provides the reader with convenience, which should *never* be underestimated. Instead of having to opt-in to twenty different forms, they opt-in once and get access to this treasure trove of useful content upgrades.

If I'm speaking at an event it's really easy to give my audience either a copy of my slides or a relevant download. Before the event, I set everything up, then use bit.ly link to change the link to something short and custom. I pop the link on my last slide, so people can snap a picture of the last slide and get the goodies when they go home.

Another thing I've done to drive sign-ups to my own list is to create a quiz. People love quizzes and they always want to know what the outcome is for them. Creating a quiz as an opt-in freebie is an awesome idea. Your quiz could be serious and in-depth or short and fun, depending on what is the best fit for your blog.

CHAPTER 22

Build your list with social media

Let's focus now on how we can build our list even more with a clever use of social media. How often do you promote that epic freebie you created as an opt-in? After the initial promotion, you might find that this post and the freebie drop off your promotion schedule, limiting the chance of email sign-ups.

I would advise that you keep track of all the posts you create, especially those with an opt-in freebie. This way you can make sure you continue to promote these posts after the initial flurry of excitement and promotion.

I use Social Oomph, which in my opinion is unrivalled, for Twitter scheduling. It allows me to schedule an initial run every few hours, then copy the tweet, change the start date and reduce the frequency. It also allows me to run a tweet indefinitely without having to input it again. Which is SUCH a time-saver!

A really easy way to drive more traffic to your freebie is to simply add your best converting or current opt-in freebie to your social media profiles.

Pinterest can be such an amazing source of traffic. However, quite often people will create a pin for the post and not mention the opt-in freebie, which is a missed opportunity. Why not create a pin telling people what the post is about and also including an image and mention of your freebie? You could even create a separate pin focusing on your opt-in and pin that too. Share that pin into group boards and into Tribes for maximum benefit.

Think about your Facebook page. Here you have several opportunities to get more email subscribers on your list. You can change the button to link people to an opt-in or to another group. Then, you can create a Facebook header image which states what your freebie is, with an image and an arrow pointing to the button. I've previously done this, and it does work.

You can also add your group to the left-hand sidebar of your page. That way people can click through and find your group from your page. Then add your opt-in link to your cover photo/video and pinned post (plus group description).

Most Facebook groups have a promo day. Simply make a spreadsheet with the groups you contribute to and their respective promo days, then you can add your link and support others too in those days. Add your opt-in call to action and link to your personal 'about' on your Facebook profile.

You can use Twitter Lead Generation Cards to collect email addresses straight from Twitter too!

Running a giveaway can be a great way to grow your subscribers a lot in a short time. However, I would recommend exercising caution when it comes to selecting an appropriate prize. Yes, you want to build your email list, BUT you only want to attract people who will be interested in your content going forward. You need to pick a product that's relevant only to your ideal audience and not the general public. If you give away an iPhone, you'll get lots of 'compers' and people who just want an iPhone. Giveaway something specific to your niche and the quality of your subscribers will increase.

I use the KingSumo Giveaways plugin, it isn't free, but it does make a difference. If an entrant shares the giveaway on their social media or with their own email list, then they have the opportunity to get even more entries into the contest. This can create a more "viral" giveaway.

What have you learned from a YouTube tutorial? I've learned to create some epic face painting designs, lots of tech stuff and countless other things. The fact that YouTube is the second largest search engine in the world should tell you something about how often it's used.

You could build your list by creating useful tutorial videos. Making sure you get them to rank and add relevant opt-in freebies to them. Write at least 300 words of content in the description box and include your keywords in this. As well as in the title and the text on your thumbnail, plus video tags, as this information will be used to rank the video. You can also add a call to action to your YouTube videos straight to your freebie link.

At the bottom of the emails you send to your list include your social sharing buttons and ask your subscribers to share. Stats show people are FAR more likely to do something if we simply ask them to. You could also ask them to forward the email to a friend and include a special opt-in form on the email.

Maybe you feel it's time to use Facebook or Pinterest ads to promote your freebie and get people onto your list that way. Paying for greater exposure certainly helps reach more people. Make sure you direct people to a dedicated opt-in page, rather than your main blog homepage. You want these new visitors only focused on one thing; joining your list.

Webinars can also be an amazing way to grow your list. The essential part of this, however, is sharing them on social media, to really increase the numbers signing up. Also making sure the people who sign up can share that they have signed up with their followers. Use multiple platforms to promote your webinar and even offer a freebie to get people to sign up or stay until the end. Promote it on all of your platforms multiple times to make sure all of your audience and potential subscribers have seen it.

Live streaming is hot property with Facebook favouring this type of video content. They can be an awesome list grower too. Create an opt-in strongly related to the subject of your Live. Then make sure you reference it multiple times, give the link (create a short memorable bit.ly link) and add the link in text too.

After the Live is completed, you can then run a Facebook video view advert for very little cost per view, which is much cheaper than standard ads. If the content and ad targeting is good enough you will hopefully get some conversions. You can retarget those who have watched a specific portion of your video (eg 25% or 50%).

Another strategy you might want to consider is to utilise gated content. This is when you lock certain content until the visitor enters their email address. You might write a post that's in two halves. You show the first half as usual but lock the second half. Then the reader can only access the rest of the content by adding their email. You then drive traffic via social media to this content. Make sure the content you are gating is worth it. It needs to be super valuable or this approach won't work. It's also a strategy not to overdo.

Each time you create a content upgrade, include a button within the PDF that your subscribers can click in order to share your freebie on Twitter. You might ask "Did you enjoy this?" Then, ask them to share by clicking a button if they did. This button then links straight to a tweet sharing the opt-in and link to sign up for it. You can use ClicktoTweet.com. I design my freebies in Canva or

Pages and in both of these programmes you can add a clickable link.

The key to growing your audience and your email list is making sure you provide consistent value. When used correctly, social media can easily take your business to the next level of profitability as a result of building your list. Make sure you keep growing your social media following, but remember that you're always trying to convert followers into subscribers.

Now, you know how important your email list is and how to grow it. I realise that the one stumbling block you might have is what to actually send to your email subscribers. What are the types of email you can send to your email list?

I send a weekly bespoke email to my list. You might want to send yours weekly or even fortnightly. Whatever you decide it's important to be consistent. You need to give them a reason to stay on your list, so make sure what you're sending them has value.

Sending worksheets, printables, checklists can be a good idea, as long as these are specific and useful your subscribers. Think of something super useful that will make their life easier.

Using a success story can be a good way to promote your affiliates. Are you an affiliate for a product you have had great success with? For example, I use, and love, the Twitter scheduler Social Oomph, so I could share my experience as a case study and obviously include my affiliate link too!

People love seeing a behind the scenes peep at your life or biz. Your emails are a great place to get a bit more personal and share more of yourself. Share these behind the scenes moments and it will help you develop the know, like and trust factor even more with your subscribers.

Another great way to bump up your affiliate income, while also serving your list with useful content, is to send a 'favourite things' email. Share a collection of your favourite books/clothes/products with them. This saves them doing the leg work in finding all these things and if they buy through your link you will earn commission!

Sharing income reports has become quite popular online. This can be a little daunting for some, but maybe you would feel happier sharing them just with your subscribers.

You might have created a 'Start here' page on your blog, but you could send an email version. This could be a great email to include in your welcome sequence, as it will help your subscribers find your best content straight out of the gate.

People are curious by nature, and as such, they're always intrigued by how others are doing. Why not share what you're doing that's growing your traffic or increasing your income. Sharing this with subscribers will certainly keep them happy. Part of my welcome sequence is an email sharing a few of my favourite tools and resources. This covers a few bases, it gives people the behind the scenes look at what I use, it helps them out with valuable recommendations (potentially saving them time) and it also generates affiliate income.

You could create a blog post that you only send to your list. This exclusive post will be a real bonus for your subscribers and it's not too difficult to create an additional weekly blog post.

A lot of what we do online is about personal connection. Telling a personal story with our audience via an email can be really effective to further develop this connection. You could tie the story you're telling in with whatever content topic you're focusing on at that particular time. Now is the time to go back to the stories swipe file you created earlier.

If you have your own products or offer services, you can provide updates via your emails. However, you could also write about updates for any brands you're an affiliate for. Do they have any new products or services you could share information on?

Why not just collate your five most popular posts and send them out as a paragraph each with a link to read the rest of the post. Chances are if they're your top posts your subscribers will enjoy them too.

Another option would be to create a seasonal round-up post. As a new season or specific time of year approaches you could send a round-up of your past seasonal posts or a collection of others which fit this time of year.

Maybe you have a fab old post that doesn't seem to get traffic anymore. You could easily take that post, give it a tweak and send it to your list. Why not try a 'How can I help you' type of email. The best way to create content is to respond to your audience's needs. Sending them an email asking for feedback on what they are struggling with or are most keen to learn about is a great idea.

You can do curated content email on any subject. For example, '5 chocolate cake recipes you must make', would be a super quick email to write, but it could also be helpful to your audience. As long as they like chocolate cake!

If you're feeling brave, you could go deep into your story. How you got where you are and the relevant bumps along the road. This will give your subscribers much more information to find things in your story that resonates with them.

Do you have any peer, influencers or friends that you could interview? We all know some pretty great people, with great stories. Why not interview them and send this interview to your list as an exclusive.

The main thing to remember when thinking about your email list content is to make sure it's helpful content. You want people to be glad they're on your list and not left wondering why they joined in the first place.

It's also important that some of the information they receive should be exclusive (only available to your list). As well as growing your email list you need to think of servicing your existing subscribers too. Regularly giving them incentives to remain on your list, after they have received their freebie. You should provide them with regular content that isn't on your blog or helpful tips and tricks. In my opinion, you should be providing this incentive content once a week.

Now you know what you're going to send, you to need to think about the subject line of your emails. If you can't get your subscribers to open your emails, it really doesn't matter how good the content in the actual email is. It could be pure gold, and no-one will ever see it if they are not compelled to open. Hence the value of a creating a compelling subject line.

It's easy to spend a lot of time crafting a great message and then just slap any old subject line on it at the end. Spending some time writing compelling email subject lines and analysing the headlines that get you the best open rates is time very well spent.

How do you create a good subject line?

Keep it short. You want your readers to see the whole subject line before they click it. Try to get your point across in fifty characters or less. Otherwise, some vital information might not be displayed.

Another great idea is to keep a swipe file of subject lines that grabbed your attention. Even if the emails are on a very different topic, you can adapt them for your own needs. I would do this by either copying them into Airtable or by simply filing them in a special email folder, so they're handy when you need inspiration.

Make sure you avoid 'spammy' words. Words like 'sale', 'discount', 'coupon', 'free', 'limited time offer' and even 'reminder' are over used and even if they don't trigger a spam filter and they do make it to your reader's inbox, chances are high that they'll get ignored.

Go back and see what subject lines got the best open rates in the past. Try to analyse why they worked well for your market. Not everything will work well in every niche. Find the types of subject lines that get your readers to open your emails and tweak from there.

While personalising emails with someone's first name has been overused in some markets, it still works well for many of us. Give it try and see if it works for you. Don't overdo it but use it when you really need them to open the email.

We're all nosey and it's hard to ignore subject lines that sound intriguing or only tell part of the story. A great psychological tool to use is the open/closed loop. When you open a loop in a subject line, the reader's mind will want to close the loop. Opening a loop could be saying something like; 'The one email trick you don't know'. Most people will click on this email as their mind really wants to close the loop and see if they do in fact know the information.

If you can evoke one or more of these feelings when your audience reads your email headlines, it will help your open rate.

- Self-Interest.
- Curiosity.
- Story.
- Social Proof.
- Humanity.
- News.
- Urgency/Scarcity.
- Offer.

Start making your swipe file today, so you're never stuck and always have inspiration. Make sure you are consciously taking note of the subject lines of the emails you receive and open. What makes you open?

ABY'S ACTION STEP

Create a new file in your inbox called email inspiration. Then every time an email lands in your inbox and it catches your attention or makes you open it. Files these away for future reference.

What makes you read a blog post or an email? Interesting stats? Witty writing? A curiosity piquing headline? All of those things can attract your interest, but they won't keep your eyes on the page on the page for long without a story. Remember when writing your weekly emails to your list you need to provide them with value AND get them to connect with you. Storytelling is such a wonderful way to ensure that they do connect with you and become a loyal reader of your emails and of your blog.

As a blogger, it's your job to craft copy that draws your reader in and keeps them interested. If you do this well, they'll identify with your message and share your content with friends and colleagues, greatly expanding your reach. Do it poorly, and they might read your post or your email. But they won't remember you in the long run because you won't have made a true connection.

One of the best ways to build a relationship and grow your audience is to share your personal stories. Tell your readers how you got started, what lessons you learned along the way, and how your life and business were improved because of them.

Our personal anecdotes don't even have to be business related to have an impact. You might have noticed a wonderful customer service trick while sitting waiting in the Doctors surgery. Share that story. Did you learn how to treat customers better by dealing with your mobile phone company? Tell your story. Making a connection between a memorable event and your business will mean your readers will remember you long after they finish reading your email.

Another powerful story telling technique you can use are case studies. Tell your readers exactly what your client did to double her income last year, or how another reader took your advice and grew her mailing list by 150% in six months or totally organised her house without any stress. These expanded testimonials will keep your readers interested in learning more from you and will show you get results. Throwing in some social proof for good measure too!

You might be able to make unusual connections in your story. Maybe your animals show you on a daily basis how important loyalty is and so you can use this story if you can easily tie it into your content. Don't chuck random stories in to your copy because you feel you should. These stories should naturally flow.

ABY'S ACTION STEP

If you haven't already got one, set up your mailing list now. If you have one on your blog (maybe built into the theme, I would advise you to export any subscribers you have in there and shut off those opt-ins. Then use a specialised service, I use Convertkit, but AWeber, MailChimp and GetResponse are also great alternatives. Import your list and then use the opt-in forms from your new service, so all your subscribers going forward get added to the list in its new location.

2016: the year I stood out.

At the end of 2016, I'd been blogging for just over three years and running my own blogging business for a large chunk of that time. During my blog-journey (X-Factor moment!) I'd gone from writing purely to capture our memories, to blogging for brands and then progressing to creating online courses for bloggers to advance their own skills. As bloggers, we're constantly learning new things about our blogs, about ourselves, our businesses and the larger online world.

2016 was a big year for me and my blog, so much happened and I really felt the energy shift in my business. I ran my first challenge, which attracted over 250 bloggers and a couple of months later I ran another one with even more bloggers involved.

In addition to my Cannes trip, I was also one of only fifteen bloggers to be invited to a Parisian blogging conference and went on a press trip to Germany as part of our Pampers ambassadorship.

I started to diversify my income streams to include courses and coaching. I launched my first e-course and sold over fifty during the initial launch. I also opened up the pre-sales for my second course, which was very well received, when it launched at the beginning of 2017.

My blog made it to number six in the Tots100 ranking of UK parenting blogs. Little did I know I would reach number one in 2017.

2016 was also the year I did my first Facebook Live and totally fell in love with it. Making it a regular part of my strategy. I grew my Twitter followers from 14.4k to 21.5k, Instagram from 4.1k to 11.4k and Pinterest from 2.5 to over 5k. The only platform that didn't go my way in terms of follower growth was Facebook.

I started to work as BritMums Social Media Manager and did my first two speaking gigs, Blog Camp and Blogfest. With regard to brand work, I signed my six biggest contracts with brands to date.

I also learned some big lessons during the year, that I want to share with you.

- Don't trade time for money. You will always lose out.
- Don't do what everyone else is doing. Go to the place your competitors won't go.

- Connecting and collaborating is MUCH more valuable than competition.
- Who you are in everyday life is who you want to be in your every-day business.
- Take imperfect action.
- We can do anything we set our minds to.
- Sometimes you can fail yourself forward.
- Embrace the things that make you unique.
- Being consistent = being successful.
- Find and embrace your people. You will always need them.
- Be open, honest and vulnerable.
- If it scares you, do it.
- Let go of guilt and embrace that you will be a powerful role model to your children.
- Value yourself and your time.
- Say no more than you say yes.
- Do what makes sense and what you love.
- Don't worry about what strangers think. They don't matter.
- Never stop learning.
- Just do one thing at any one time.
- Do your own thing.
- Keep moving forward.
- A task expands to fit the time given for its completion (OK so this is Parkinson's Law, but I had to get it in!).
- If your goals don't make you feel uncomfortable, they aren't big enough.
- Automate anything that you do repeatedly.
- Focus on building your email list rather than your social media followers.
- Don't limit yourself. You can do great things.

- People buy from people they know, like and trust.
- The best time to act is before you're ready.
- Serve first, ask later.
- Nothing worth having is ever easy.
- You can't do everything on your own.
- We will never have more time, we just need more focus.
- You don't have to be an expert to teach, you just have to know more than the people you intend to teach.
- Just do it.
- We all have a superpower, we just have to find out what it is.
- Good marketing is using the exact words your audience uses.
- Write for your true fans, not for traffic.
- Use Facebook ads to validate your idea.
- Be confident and kind (arrogance is not confidence. Arrogance is being dismissive of others).

Standing out in a crowd

2016 was definitely the year I felt like I started to gain more traction and get noticed.

You start a blog, spend time designing it and creating posts; then you want more. You want your blog to be exposed to a larger audience. You want it to be noticed. However, with hundreds of new blogs being started everyday how can you make your blog stand out. How do you rise above the masses and get enough traction to take your blog to the next level?

First things first, and this might be obvious, but you need to 'be you'. As I've said many times, readers connect with real people and they will come back to hear your story. It's important to show them who you really are. There's only one of you, so that's your USP, tap into it, that will be the reason people will come back to your blog.

Make sure you write quality posts. Again, it should be obvious, but all your posts should serve a purpose; share your family life, preserve your memories, solve a reader's problem or provide a service, but they should do something. Writing about a trip to the supermarket, for example, would tick none of these boxes (unless there was an angle).

Before you hit publish think, is there a point to this post? Am I trying to educate, entertain or inspire? Creating content that does one of these things will ensure people keep coming back.

Visuals are so important to a blog. I will be honest, I can click on a blog and click straight back off it if I don't like the aesthetics. I'm so disappointed if I like the content, but I find the blog is visually unappealing. Does that make me shallow? Probably, but there are so many competing blogs, that to capture my attention for a return visit or possibly a mention on my blog, the blog really has to be the full package. Good visuals include both graphics for post titles and photography. Avoid dark, small images, they really aren't appealing.

Working with other bloggers is beneficial in so many ways as we delved into earlier. Collaborations are a great way to become involved in the community side of blogging, they can increase your traffic and ultimately increase your following.

If you skipped over the design stuff at the start of this book, now's the time to go back and soak that up. You need to take time to select the right theme for your blog. This is more than just aesthetics; you need a theme that is attractive, yes, but functional is so important too. There are free themes, but for a small amount of money (mine was $50) you can purchase a theme that you can customise to a greater extent than with the free options. If people come to your blog and have a tough time navigating, they won't go away talking about you for the right reasons.

I personally feel that in most cases the majority of text on your site should be black with a light-coloured background. You can always have colourful accents to add to your personality. Your blog needs to look professional and not give people a headache when they are trying to read a post. Just because you like orange and purple doesn't mean your posts have to be written in those colours. Read other blogs and see which ones you enjoy reading more from a visual point of view, this might give you some ideas of what would work for your blog.

Blogging can take up lots of your time and it can be easy to focus on solely your own blog. However, no one is going to notice you if you do that. You need to comment on other people's posts and have conversations on social media. Why not retweet people's content or share on your Facebook page, but make sure it is meaningful and genuine? I've made lots of connections and amazing friends through social media and commenting on other people's blogs.

One of my best friends, Amy, came to my attention because she started to leave lovely, meaningful comments on my blog. She stuck in my mind, I visited her blog and we struck up a friendship, that turned out to be one of the best gifts blogging has given me.

Make sure you go self-hosted as early as you can. To earn money, and to signal to people that you are serious, your blog needs to be self-hosted (if on WordPress). As soon as I went self-hosted, PRs and brands started to approach me.

Getting your blog noticed by other bloggers, readers and brands does take time and quite a lot of effort. Not everyone can write a post that goes viral. Most of us have to build our networks one step at a time.

CHAPTER 24

How do you build your online credibility?

As an influencer it's so important to build up great relationships with your audience and develop a community around your blog in order to build up credibility. Ultimately, we need people to listen to what we have to say. Whether that is because we will be sharing a brand's message or sharing our own products and content. The goal is to be listened to.

Sharing amazing FREE information that gets your readers results will be a great way to start building trust. Show up regularly and be reliable in the content you create and they will begin to know you and share your true self and this credibility will start to develop.

If your audience consists of four people, one of which is your mum, then it doesn't really matter too much how credible you are to them. This isn't a large enough audience to allow you to gain traction and momentum.

For this you need a volume of people… you need traffic. So, you need to focus on where your traffic comes from? Which platform is your biggest referrer? Is it Twitter, if so get over there and make sure your opt-ins are well represented in your tweets. Ask friends to retweet a tweet about your latest opt-in, pin the tweet, do whatever you can to capitalise on your best traffic source.

Is there something topical that has gone viral or at least done well on another Facebook page? If so why not share it on your page? Invite those extra likers and hopefully, they will come over to your blog for a nosy. Then keep working round all your traffic sources making sure you are pimping out your opt-ins on these platforms.

Keep an eye on your analytics — Google Analytics can give you so much information. Information that can help you make decisions and shape your blog going forward. Find out which topics your audience loves the most and which topics don't seem to resonate with them.

Social media is such an incredibly powerful marketing tool that can make it possible for you to reach a potentially unlimited number of people with little investment in terms of time, money and effort.

While social media might be incredibly powerful, it's still only going to be as good as the strategy you have in place. You'll find that if you haven't first established yourself as a credible authority, then everything you do will fall on deaf ears.

So, your blog is now filled with well-researched, in-depth and informative posts (with great opt ins) and you're sharing them on social media. These are the basics of content marketing and one of the best ways to establish trust, authority and credibility in your niche.

Even if you base yourself on Facebook or maybe you're a big Instagrammer, having a blog means you have a home base that you're in control of.

Unfortunately, if you have a social media account with fourteen followers, you'll have a tricky time persuading people to put much value in what you say. Of course, it shouldn't necessarily matter, but it does. As a result of social proof, people often see follower numbers as an indicator of your authority, so get to work growing those followers – but remember always transition these people to your list!

We all like to know that there's a real human being behind a social media account. Showing your real personality can help to build trust and therefore credibility. Every now and then posting a personal image will help to build that connection with your fans. Automation is fine and totally recommended, but make sure you put some personal interaction in your strategy somewhere.

It's good to be personal, but not too personal... a drunken rant or a tweet about your personal life can also seriously undermine your respectability and will dent your credibility. You might think it's amusing or poignant, but your business account is not the place for that kind of content. Make sure your social media pages have strong branding that utilises great quality images and well-written copy.

Credibility comes, in part, from consistency. Posting regularly and showing up for your audience will go a long way. If you go days, weeks or months on end without posting then your social media will look like a ghost town, suggesting it's not a professional account. Focus on creating *consistent* content on your blog and on social media.

Assumed credibility can also be very useful. If another authority in your niche recommends you or gives you a shout-out, you will assume some of their credibility in the eyes of their followers.

ABY'S ACTION STEP

Go to Google Analytics and find out which ten posts rank the highest for you in terms of traffic? Then brainstorm an opt-in freebie for each one. Remember, these opt-ins should be congruent to the post and what you feel the reader will need next or something that will make their life easier.

Treat your blog like a business before it is a business

Most of us start our blogs as a hobby; maybe something to pass the time or a way to capture our family memories (as I did). Often they can develop into something else; our jobs or a way to make us some extra money.

Either way, whether your blog is a major part of your income or a much-loved hobby, there are some things that you really should invest in. You would be lucky to take up any hobby and not have to buy the equipment to enable you to take part. You certainly couldn't run a business without making some investments.

Try to focus on what you think you need, don't be seduced by things other bloggers are spending their money on. It might work for them, but it doesn't necessarily mean it will do the same for you. So keep your own needs in mind when spending your money. I've bought so much stuff over the years that I didn't need, the strangest being a drone that ironically doesn't fly...

There are certain things which are a great investment. Having a custom domain will make your blog look much more professional to the outside world. It will give the impression to readers and PRs that you are serious about your blog. I think back in the day mine was £19.00, but you might be able to find one for around $1.00; either way it won't break the bank.

If your site is not self-hosted, it needs to be. It can seem a bit scary, but it really isn't that difficult to make the change and most hosting companies will do it for you if you will be using them for your hosting. Moving to self-hosted also gives you much more control over the theme you use, the design options and you can add amazing plug-ins to your blog, which will help you more than you can imagine. There are various hosting companies and basic hosting usually starts at around £2.99 per month.

I think it's worth investing in your branding. Your brand ties together your blog, social media platforms and so you want to get it right. You might DIY at the start but at some point, I think it's a great investment to make. This might be in the form of a logo or a complete design package. In an ideal world, you want people to be able to catch a glimpse of a header or a profile and know it's your brand. That immediate recognition, which will go a long way to making your brand seem more professional, authoritative and cohesive.

As we've explored, the design of your blog is such an important factor. It can be the difference between someone landing on your blog and bouncing straight off or hanging around and becoming a regular reader.

I would always advise people to purchase social media schedulers to help you boost their social media presence. As well as growing your blog, you need to simultaneously grow your social profiles, so they support each other. This growth will make brands sit up and take notice.

Most bloggers use multiple social platforms and it can be exhausting, impossible even, to keep on top of them all. I always say you have to be on them all, but you don't have to win them all. I pick one to devote lots of time to (whichever I want to grow at that current time), then I will work on another two to a lesser extent and tick over the others (mainly with auto-posting).

You need to share your posts on social media to make sure your content is getting the attention it deserves. However, scheduling all your content can be so time-consuming. I think you need to spend your time on networks to engage, but let a scheduler take the strain with the scheduling and distributing your posts. After all, it doesn't make any difference if you do this manually or if a scheduler does it for you. The engagement is where it's at, so save your time to do that.

It's false economy not to use schedulers, because they are a few pounds a week. They will save you hours of inputting and will free up so much time so you have more time to earn, write content or just be with your family. My schedulers save me hours each week.

So, if you're starting to think about where to invest some cash, these are the areas that I would recommend injecting even a small amount of money into. Once you have these areas under control, the landscape of your blog and how it's perceived will change immeasurably for the better.

CHAPTER 25

Bloggers rock! Please realise your worth.

Bloggers are hot property, whether they blog about food, fashion, family, lifestyle or one of the countless other niches; bloggers can now be global influencers. I don't know about you, but I find that hugely exciting.

Many of us started our blogs as a hobby and have watched them develop into something much more than that. Something that in some cases provides us with a good living and very exciting opportunities. Despite the prominence and value of bloggers, there are still bloggers who don't seem to value what they do, well, not enough anyway. We all should realise our worth. Whether we're earning from our blogs, plan to in the future or simply write to help others or to document our lives; we're all important and all have the opportunity to positively influence people through our blogs.

I shared with you earlier in this book my moment of realisation. It came on that plane journey to Monaco.

This is why you need your moment of realisation.

We juggle. Most bloggers balance blogging with other things. Be that paid employment away from the home or simply the demands of being a parent, it's a constant juggle and we all do it.

We don't just do it, we achieve great things too. Our voices have made a real difference. Bloggers have raised vast amounts of money for charity (Team Honk, Save Syrian Children), helped to change laws, raised the profile for various causes and made people feel like they are not alone, the value of which should never be underestimated. My lovely friend Emma (Brummy Mummy of 2) has even done the voiceover in animated film! We do all that while doing countless other tasks too.

We hustle. As bloggers, it's rare that a brand comes along and offers us a lovely opportunity on a plate. In most cases, we hustle and work contacts. We are self-starters that make things happen. This is not always easy, but day after day we do it.

We are creative. When we work with brands we creatively produce awesome content. Many of us produce videos or put an unusual spin on the content we produce. We don't just write basic posts. We create engaging content to highlight the brands we are working with. The creativity of bloggers never ceases to amaze me.

We are jacks of all trades and master of SO MANY too! Most businesses have different departments. They have finance, IT, HR, at the very least. Yet within our blogs we are all these things. If we have a financial issue we can't just fob it off on John in Finance, we have to learn how to deal with it ourselves. If we don't know how to do something we learn. This attitude results in us having a wide range of skills including photography, videography, financial management, IT, social media, PR, the works!

When we post content on our blog it has longevity, unlike a newspaper which will be tomorrow's chip wrapping. These posts, whether they are a week old or a year old, can still be searched for and found by readers. This should be valued; a brand can reap the benefit of a post years after it has gone live.

We are both consumer and promoter. When we write about a product, we are seen as both a consumer and a promoter. The brand itself is seen as simply the promoter, but readers know that we are individuals who make our own purchasing decisions. Although we may be acting on behalf of a brand, we are seen as more 'human' than the brand, which often means we are trusted more. Our readers know we are honest and wouldn't promote something that we wouldn't buy ourselves.

Building social networks takes time and effort. Say a company wants you to tweet something out and you know it will only take a couple of minutes, do you do it for free? The length of time it will take is irrelevant; the point is that it might have taken you years to build your social following and that is what the brand should be paying for, not whether it's a quick job or not.

As a blogger, your readers invest their time in following your life and because of this investment in time they often feel as if they know you. As a result of this assumed closeness, they trust your advice. With this trust comes a responsibility to be honest and transparent with what we recommend on our blogs, so that we respect the trust of our readers.

Research (MuseFind.com) has found that 92% of consumers trust an influencer more than an advertisement or traditional celebrity endorsement. I know I've bought things after I have spotted them on a blog (hello Saltwater sandals!).

People are more trusting of bloggers than of newspaper articles, which they assume will be less objective. Among consumers aged 18-34, blogs were the number one most valued resource in making a purchasing decision, above friends and family, which is the most valued resource for anyone over the age of 35 (researchnow.co.uk). Interesting stuff!

Consumers want to learn about a brand from a third party, not directly from the brand. A brand will be perceived as biased, but a third party who knows about the brand and likes it enough to choose to promote it, is very powerful.

We are niche. Unlike traditional publishers our audience is really targeted, so brands can reach their exact market, rather than wasting resources targeting a more general population who may or may not be interested in their product.

As bloggers, we are classed as 'mid-level influencers'. Not huge influencers like Beyoncé, no we occupy the middle of the spectrum. Studies (such as the Musefind.com study) show that mid-level influencers influence the buying public more readily than the top-flight influencers. I bet you didn't know you're more influential than Beyoncé!

As you can see, we ALL rock! So, believe it and next time someone asks you what you do, stand proud and tell them you're a blogger.

The next time someone asks you to work for free, you know what to say. Value yourself and demand fair pay for your skills.

ABY'S ACTION STEP

I want you to create your own worthiness affirmation. Affirmations can be really useful to centre us and ground us back into reality when we start to feel detached from reality. Here are some examples.

- *I am worthy to receive all that I ask.*
- *I deserve a life full of achievement, love and success.*
- *I honour and value my worth.*
- *I welcome those experiences and successes. I deserve all that I receive.*

Saying 'NO' could be the best thing for your blog

There will come a time in your journey that overwhelm will hit. You'll have taken on too many reviews and you will be wondering why you thought you needed all this stuff in the first place. You agreed because you were thrilled to be asked, but now you're spending so many hours trying to get through all the work before you can post that review, it doesn't seem as positive an experience as you thought it would be.

There's one word that us bloggers should use more and that's 'no'. It seems that lots of us seem a little too grateful for every opportunity that comes our way. Regardless of whether it's a good opportunity or not. Or whether it's a good fit for our blog or not. Someone has asked us to collaborate and often we feel compelled to say, 'yes'. It never feels good to disappoint people and we all love to be helpful. So even when we should say no, often we say yes.

What I want to talk about how empowering saying, 'no' can be and how that one little word could be the best thing for you and your blog. Why we all need to be a little more Meghan Trainor, 'My name is, no. My sign is, no. My number is, no'.

Saying, 'no' isn't a negative thing. In fact, it can be just the opposite. It can leave you open to receive other 'better fitting' opportunities.

Just because we physically can do something, doesn't mean we should do it.

The simple fact is that your blog will actually stop growing if you're afraid of saying no. That might sound a bit odd, but if you fill your time up with projects and collaborations that you don't really want to do and that won't move the needle forward. You'll be spending all your time and energy for nothing. As a result, you'll have nothing left to grow your blog, collaborate on the projects you do want to do and move your blog forward. Saying no might feel awkward, but it will stop you drowning under a workload of things you aren't ultimately going to benefit from.

Being your own boss means that you can pick and choose who you work with. Yes, we could all say we need the money from such potential collaborations but working with someone you don't get along with is going to make you dread your work. I'm pretty sure that's not why you started working for yourself. So my advice — go with your gut instinct. Do you think you will be able to work happily with this person? If you don't then don't accept the collaboration.

I adore helping other people and would never want people to be apprehensive about asking for help. However, sometimes we can fall into patterns of behaviour and accepted norms where people come to you for help before trying to help themselves. Which can be a little frustrating. In order for others to value your time, YOU need to value your own time.

It's not personal. It's just business. You know what's best for your blog. If you don't think something is a good fit for you and your blog, recommend another blogger who may be interested. The PR will thank you and the other blogger will be glad of the opportunity.

Saying 'no' needs to flow over into your non-work life too. Are you over-run with invitations and commitments? It's time to say 'no' at home too, reclaim some of that time to enjoy and relax your home-life. Don't waste hours at a party you don't want to go to, just say no. I've done this so many times! Value what you want to do and make sure you're not just agreeing on things just to make others happy. You're important too.

You need to protect your time. No-one will do this for you. Consider the last review you were offered; did you really want the product? When you add up the time it took to review the item, take the photos, write up the post, proof-read it; was it worth it?

Remember you only have a limited amount of energy, so you need to use that time wisely.

If you say yes to most things you are offered, you can be compromising your blog and your brand. Choose quality over quantity, so you have the space to produce the best possible content for the brands you work with.

Having too many commitments can lead to you dropping the ball and producing content that you are not 100% pleased with. Being more selective can give you more time to create the best content you can, which reflects your professionalism.

It's worth stating that saying no doesn't have to be negative or appear rude. If you decline an opportunity explain why and offer recommendations of other suitable bloggers.

Saying no doesn't mean the PR or brand won't want to work with you again. If you handle it correctly they will remember you for being honest and helpful.

ABY'S ACTION STEP

It's time to decide on some boundaries. Going forward, what are you going to say no to? Will it be collaborations under a certain monetary value? Or a certain type of collaborations? Maybe you will commit to not working past 9.00 pm or never working at the weekend. What makes sense for you?

Niching down to smash your goals.

If your blog is more than a hobby, then blogging goals are very important. With blogging comes an endless list of tasks that need doing, plus you'll most likely have lots of ideas that you want to explore and perhaps implement. Without goals, you might find that you don't feel as if you're moving forward and growing your blog.

Goals help you stay motivated and can drive you forward if you hit a blogger's slump! However, a problem may arise if you decide one of your goals is the hit 200k Pinterest followers in the next six months when your current followers are 500. You probably wouldn't achieve this, which could then leave you feeling despondent and deflated, as if you had failed, when the truth is that you didn't fail, your goal was just unrealistic in the first place.

Goal setting is a really important thing to do for both yourself and your business. By setting goals, we're more likely to stay focused and determined to achieve. We also want to be sure that our plans leave us time to enjoy life and not chase our tails on tasks that might not contribute to our end goals.

How do you set effective goals? Goals that you won't just write down and promptly forget about?

I always start by thinking about what matters most to me. Whether that's a financial aim, completing a particular project, or even where you see your business in five years' time. Then think about what success looks like to you. We all have a different definition of success and as long as you know what yours is you're just fine.

I've also found that it can be really useful to have a word of the year. This word sums up how you want to show up during that twelve months. It's usually a reflection of what you want to achieve. Previous words for me have been focus, brave, and more recently, exposure.

ABY'S ACTION STEP

Let's get your mission clear before we start.

[YOUR BLOG] helps [YOUR IDEAL READER] to [WHAT THEY WANT TO ACHIEVE] so that they [THEIR CORE DESIRE]

Now you know what you need to do, how are you going to achieve it?

"To accomplish this goal I will:_____"
"To accomplish this goal I will never:_____"

These two statements really sum up your ethos and the values of your brand. It maybe that you will balance free and paid content and you will never take your audience for granted. Whatever rings true for you.

Grab a piece of paper or your favourite notebook and brain dump everything you want to achieve in life, blog and everything else. Don't censor yourself (we do too much of that) just write.

Next, you're going to highlight the projects you want to achieve in the next twelve months. These should be your large goals, sometimes called **Outcome goals.** They won't be your ultimate super long-term ones. Just focus on the next twelve months. I don't want to be too prescriptive on how many you choose but aim for roughly seven-ten. They must be achievable with effort.

Did you know you're 42% (Matthews) more likely to achieve your goals if you write them down regularly? *I know, 42%*!

'Thoughts disentangle themselves passing over the lips and pencil tips' - Anon

Life often takes over and so our outcome goals need to be kept somewhere prominent. This will mean we will see them every day and they'll become lodged in our consciousness.

If we believe something will happen or that we will achieve something, it's MUCH more likely to happen, because we MAKE it so. Also, because we focus our efforts on those goals primarily, we are less likely to get side-tracked.

Here's the plot twist!

We aren't going to focus on our entire year. Instead, we're going to divide all of your annual goals into ninety-day cycles. Breaking your year down into ninety-day cycles makes so much more sense for a few reasons.

Psychologically it's hard for us to work for something which our brain considers too far into the future. Todd Herman found that ninety days ahead is the magical horizon, past which our mind switches off a little. Goals within a ninety-day window are seen as goals which can impact our 'today' and therefore, are readily achieved.

You should definitely have a long-term vision, but this isn't something tangible that you are working on directly right now. Your efforts should be focused on developing skills that will have the most impact on your business.

Ninety-day goals are far less overwhelming than standard annual goals. They also allow you to be more agile and can change your course if necessary. Your motivation will be higher and so you will be more focused and productive. You can set goals for later in the year depending on your year so far.

Analyse each outcome goal. When will you make this

happen? Also, add in your financial expectations for each. Don't be shy, it's important to commit to a figure, as this will mean you are more likely to achieve it. Without committing to a number we're just going with the flow and leaving it up to chance and fate, which is no way to run a business.

The next step is to assign your key outcome goals to points on your yearly calendar. For example, I want to run four free challenges during the year, it would make sense for me to put one free challenge in each ninety-day cycle. Allocate all your goals in this way and write them on your calendar where it makes sense for them to be.

Only focusing on your first ninety-day cycle. Work backwards from each outcome goal and add in your smaller milestone goals (performance goals) at appropriate times, which will lead you to success and achievement of your main outcome goals.

Need an example? If one of my outcome goals was to sell fifty spots on a course. The performance goals could be:

- Finish creating the course
- Grow my email list so I can reach more people.
- Advertise the course on Facebook.
- Use social media to create interest.
- Open sign-ups.

I would then take each one of these goals and break them into the smallest actions they can be. Resulting in our process goals. These are the things you put on your to-do list.

How else can you stack the odds in your favour when it comes to goal achievement? One great trick is to reward yourself for your achievements. Treat yourself to something you want when you achieve one of your goals. These rewards will help you stay focused and motivated. You could even tie the reward to the goal. So, for example, if your goal was photography based, then the reward could be something new for your camera.

Depending on your personality type, you might find having a tribe to hold you accountable could be really useful. I'm an Obliger, so I need outside accountability in order for me to meet my own goals.

Gretchen Rubin writes, "To meet inner expectations, Obligers must create structures of outer accountability. They need tools such as supervision, late fees, deadlines, monitoring, and consequences enforced from the outside to keep their promises to themselves."

Finding a small group of like-minded people, within which you can share your goals can help immeasurably. You can all hold each other accountable and help each other make progress on your goals.

To give yourself maximum chance of success you need to review your goals frequently. Know your goals well and revisit them regularly. Even if it's just a little check in to see how you're getting on. This will re-motivate and refocus you, also giving you a reminder of the work still to do.

Sometimes achieving our goals takes a mindset shift too. Who will you need to become to achieve your goals? If your goals are a little hairy-scary and they're going to take lots of networking for example, you'll need to be a confident person who can engage others. Are you? If not, you need to become that person if you're to succeed.

This might seem more complicated than traditional goal setting. However, ask yourself, how many times has traditional long-term goal setting failed you? I'm guessing a few times. Setting goals this way might take a little longer to start with, but you will have a huge amount of focus, you will always be working on things that will have a positive impact on your outcome goals and you will eventually have more precious family time.

ABY'S ACTION STEP

Decide on your seven-ten *outcome goals for the next year. Divide these into quarters, depending on what fits best where in your year. Then break these goals down into sub-goals and then the smallest tasks that go on your to-do list. Oh, and put them on your to-do list!*

Niche, the common resistance

Imagine two shops side-by-side in a shopping centre. One is your go-to shop for just about everything. They sell garden tools, kitchenware, sweets, t-shirts, car parts, baby clothes, oh and apples. The other is more exclusive. In fact, the only thing they sell is chocolate; expensive Swiss chocolate of all variations. If it's not chocolate, you won't find it in that shop.

At first glance, it might seem as if the chocolate shop is limiting its revenue potential. There are so many other things they could add in terms of complimentary stock, such as non-chocolate gifts and cards?

In reality if you think the sell-a-bit-of-everything shop has more potential, you'd be wrong. When you clarify and reduce the focus of your offerings to be left with only those which closely match your business goals, you will be in a far better position to attract your ideal client. It doesn't end there though you'll have customers lining up to pay a premium for your services.

The sell everything shop will have more customers, as well, they sell everything! They are selling so many things that by necessity their prices have to be lower. There is no customer loyalty here, just people seeking bargains!

The chocolate shop is different. They have fewer customers, but their clients are far more loyal. They spend more money and they tell their friends about the awesome chocolate shop they found.

See how this affects your business? As a blogger, it's critical for you to know exactly what you want to provide, and to whom. If you simply create a big old mix of products without a clear direction, you might make a few sales (especially if you price on the low end) but you won't gain a loyal following. Your customers are only motivated by price and so they will always be looking for a bargain.

All your products should fit with your brand and should instantly tell new visitors exactly what you do. Take a look at your current products and get rid of those which are on the edges of what your core message is. Focus on your core products and work to make them better and more valuable. Your loyal following will then develop. It's time to stop being the pound shop!

Many of you reading this book will be in the family lifestyle or parenting niche. If you're thinking of making an income from products, then a niche will help you focus on which products you can sell.

Your niche often comes from your superpower. It's an extension of this — the practical application. It is the thing you want to be known for. You might write a parenting blog, but what do you answer the majority of questions about? Maybe you've got great content on allergies or breastfeeding. What is it that people come to you for? Which topic are you on authority in? That right there is your niche.

I really believe that most people, if not ALL people, have a niche, they just haven't found it yet. Most of us have something we can sell and something that we can give advice on. Whether you're a brilliant designer and could sell beautiful downloads. Or maybe you're really good at giving people advice and have been through a lot in your life, in which case, maybe a self-help e-book would be the product for you. There's a product in all of us.

Now, it might take you a while to figure out what your product should be, what your superpower is and which specific niche you fit into. You might be able to do this on your own or you might need some guidance. Either way, when you figure out the answers to these questions you will have a clear picture of which area you should be focusing on.

You need to make sure you have a solid foundation on which you can build this new facet of your business. You now know the main niche, but you need to dig deeper to find out exactly how your product should be positioned.

The information product business is competitive and the best way to make it in this business is to cater to a specific group of people who have a problem that needs solving. This means you have to find your niche market. Niche markets are not difficult to identify, you just need to do a little research and use a lot of common sense.

Start by writing a list of all the areas and topics you have some knowledge about. Don't worry about not being an 'expert' on the topic; remember what I said about being one step ahead of the people you're teaching?

Brainstorm what you love to talk about. What are your passions? (e.g. knitting, keeping fit, healthy eating). Then think about who you like to help the most; what groups of people do you identify with? (new mums, women working in corporate). What issues do this group of people have? What do they need help with? (are they are short of time, feeling stressed, don't get enough sleep, want to be fitter or lose weight).

Then you can mix these up to get various combinations making up possible niches. For example, maybe you help corporate women de-stress by teaching them to knit. Or maybe you help new mums to eat healthily by helping them create five minute recipes. You get the idea.

When you're confident with your niche, don't get stressed when you spot someone else doing exactly what you've just decided to do. This is just proof that there is a need, it's validation. No one ever has a truly original idea, but your execution and personality make your version unique.

While it might feel exciting to try to find a niche unicorn, often sticking to tried and tested ones is the best way to go. These niches, such a weight loss and parenting aren't going anywhere, and people will always need help in these areas. People are always going to want to lose weight and they're not going to stop having kids either!

If you're going for one of these wider niches, then just focus on a micro niche within this main area. For example, instead of targeting general weight loss, why not aim at new mums or women going through menopause? By choosing a smaller targeted group you stand a much better chance of succeeding with your products.

Research is everything. Before you start creating content and products it's important to plan and ensure there's a viable market for your product. You can get lots of great information about your niche from simply popping over to Amazon.

Look at books in your chosen niche and focus on the reviews that are between two-four stars. What was the feedback? What did the readers like? What did they dislike, or feel was left out? This gives you a great start to ensuring your product (whatever form it takes!), will be giving the people what they want.

I would suggest that you keep it simple at the start. The most important thing is that you start. It can be easy to focus on every small detail and end up not moving forward at all.

'Winners take imperfect action while losers are still perfecting the plan' - Tony Robbins.

A great way to overcome this is to make everything easy. Don't worry about other products or your systems, just get started. All you really need is a simple sales page, a product and a way to sell it. Payhip is a really easy and great option for selling your products. You can be set up in as little as ten minutes and they handle all the payment processing for you.

Remember, there's plenty of time to get more complex later. Your business will continue to grow, so for now just make it happen then refine things later. Your main goal right now is to **just do it**.

Don't stop, keep going. Once you're finished creating and setting up your product to sell, things are just getting started! Now you need to market your product. You need to get the word out about your product. Utilise your connections, your social media following and your blog to promote this product.

Info products are a way of packaging up your knowledge and selling it to someone in an easy to handle the format. This knowledge could be teaching someone something new or simply making their life easier. Either way they will be adding value to the purchaser's life in some way.

Don't underestimate the value of the knowledge you have. I've heard so many people over the years say things like, 'Well it's nothing they couldn't get for free on the internet'. Newsflash! You can pretty much learn anything you want for free on the internet. But people pay for your experience, they pay for your particular take on the information, they pay for you to assimilate the information and give it to them in bite-sized pieces. They pay for convenience.

They pay for you to be the shortcut.

Passive income through the sale of your own products is a brilliant way to make money from your blog, which is not ultimately reliant on brands choosing you to work with them.

It's important to think about serving your community first and foremost. You need to give them lots of free value before they will even consider buying a product from you. Plus you need to keep on nurturing them even if they never buy your product.

ABY'S ACTION STEP

What do you audience need help with? Brainstorm the areas you could provide solutions in and then drill down and think about specific products you could offer. What format makes the most sense for your audience? E-book, audio course, full, detailed course?

CHAPTER 27

Bring on the brands.

When I started blogging I had no idea how to work with brands, none, squat, nadda! I saw everyone else doing it and I felt like I would never be able to turn my hobby blog into a business — I didn't even know where to start. I was so overwhelmed and realised I needed way more skills to be able to capitalise on this potential new income stream.

I needed a system, hell, I just needed some information about how to get work with brands. I wrote so many pretty rubbish emails in my early months, which probably cost me a few jobs along the way. I didn't know how to value my blog and negotiate and was frustrated to hear bloggers securing more money for the same campaigns that I'd done.

A lot of what matters most is negotiation and positioning; done right this will ensure you get jobs and get paid what you're worth. Over the years I have honed my skills and have worked with some pretty pukka brands if I do say so myself. I've travelled abroad multiple times and had super exciting experiences, while also earning a good income too. ALL from my couch and *mostly* while wearing n onesie... I'm a comfort girl what can I say!

Is it possible to work with brands when you're a new blogger?

There are so many brands that want to work with bloggers and they don't ALL want to work with big, established bloggers. As a new blogger or one with a smaller following, you might be under the assumption that brands won't want to connect with you. You aren't influential enough and you don't have a big enough audience. That's simply not true. Even if you're a micro-influencer (a content creator with less than 10k followers) you can still secure work with brands.

All content creators should know what they bring to the table, but as a smaller blogger, you should 'own' and be able to shout from the rooftops what you can offer the brand. What can you do for them that they can't do for themselves? It might be that you have a super-engaged Facebook page, maybe a thriving Instagram community or a real skill for video content creation. If you have lower stats, then you ideally need something to offer instead. At this point, if you don't have anything, you may need to build up your stats, skills, and community before reaching out to brands.

If you're a micro-influencer who has this extra skill or attractive factor, then you're hot property! Brands are becoming more and more interested in the power of smaller influencers and are keen to collaborate with them. Again, this goes back to your audience believing you.

Unlike celebrities, who are also paid to endorse things; your audience is more genuinely connected to you. They will believe that you're coming from a good place and not just in it for the money. Micro-influencers can often benefit from more organic reach than higher level influencers and celebrities. This translates to more eyeballs on your content and more exposure for the brand.

Often micro-influencers have a narrower niche and narrow niches help specific groups of people solve a problem. So, you can become more of an authority within this narrow niche than you would achieve within a wider niche. If this narrow niche is right for the brand, they will be super excited to work with you.

Whether you're a micro-influencer or a larger influencer, there are certain things that brands will look for. They want to work with bloggers who stand out in some way. It's important that you show your personality through your blog. No-one wants to work with Beige Bev! Show your personality and you will attract your audience, who will love what you do.

These people will become regular readers and this engagement is what the brand is looking for. Think about showing your personality, but with professionalism. If a brand checked your social media channels, would you be worried?

It's important to show brands how your audience matches the demographic the brand wants to tap into. Show the company how you fit with their brand and how your audience does too. Why would your audience be interested in their particular brand?

Stats are important to most brands, BUT they aren't the most important thing in all cases. When you're a new blogger your stats might not be huge, however, there are newer brands that are small themselves who may be a perfect fit for you. Even larger brands may love what you do and want to partner with you.

Just be confident about your stats and what you have to offer. You could show the brand how your stats are growing a certain percentage each month and you could even include a testimonial from a brand you have previously worked with. Stats don't always give the whole picture and so it's really important to focus on engagement and producing quality content.

When we contact a brand, the representative will probably click the links you provide to get an impression of your blog. Try to avoid too many sponsored and review posts. Instead, try to mix your sponsored work with organic content. Also, try to avoid lots of short posts (under 400 words). These don't really give much value to your audience and they're not great for SEO either. Poor graphics, a lack of disclosure and bad spelling and grammar will all be off-putting. Instead try to focus on substantial posts, which are useful to your audience. Work on your post layout and graphics. Making sure you link to and showcase other relevant posts you have.

Brands often need us bloggers for exposure to a certain demographic. This means knowing who your readers are is really important. You will need to know your monthly page views, unique users, where your audience live, their gender and age brackets. Possibly even their education and/or income levels (although these two are less commonly required).

Brands are interested in engagement and with the ever-changing algorithms engagement, in many cases, has suffered. For me Instagram has been the most affected. A lot of my friends comment that they never see my pictures in their feed and my analytics show that my images are shown to around 300 people in my audience, despite having around 17k followers! I've never bought followers, but I do not have hour upon hour each day to spend engaging on Instagram in order to increase the likes on my pictures. So, as you can see engagement can be difficult for many reasons. Some brands might be looking for a particular engagement ratio to work with you. However, these are not set in stone.

Brands will also be looking at the comments and will be assessing whether they think you can influence your audience.

You might have got into blogging to write and may think photos are not too important. However, to brands good quality original imagery (and video if relevant) are really important. They want to be associated with a quality blog, and if they are sending you products they want to know you will take good pictures of them.

It's useful to have a media kit, which is really like a CV for your blog. In this, ideally one-page, document you can outline the elevator pitch for your blog, the demographics of your audience, your blogging achievements, the collaborations you offer, followers and traffic numbers. You might not always be asked for one, but they're important when pitching and it does make you look more prepared and professional. You don't have to put rates on your media kit and I would actually advise against it. Each campaign will have differences in the deliverables required and so it's a better idea to give a custom price for each campaign.

If you want to take the initiative and reach out to brands, the most important factors of any pitch are that it's clear, concise and relevant. Brands do not need an essay. Be clear on what you want and what you offer in return. Don't make the brand try to figure out where you could fit into their marketing plan, do that for them. Show them how the demographics of your readers fit their desired audience.

Be confident in your worth. As a blogger, chances are you have an engaged and trusting audience. Your readers feel as if they know you. They've read stories about your family's happy and sad times; maybe even watched your children grow up. They trust you and value your opinion. This is a lot more appealing to brands than you think. They are looking more and more towards bloggers to promote their products.

I'm exceptionally grateful for the opportunities my family and I've had. We have been on lots of incredible holidays, had many fab days out, been for lovely meals, received fantastic goods, worked as brand ambassadors, earned cold hard cash and have built many fantastic relationships with wonderful companies.

My advice is to be flexible and think outside the box in terms of what you can offer. If a company or a PR emails you, think of ways you can work together. For example, if they are not offering enough money for you to create a post, offer to do some social media promotion instead.

Don't delete press releases! I've lost count of the amount of times I hear people saying they just delete the press releases sent to them. DON'T! I know they're sent out in a blanket fashion, but you can still use them as a conversation starter. Email back and ask the PR if they are looking for sponsored content or reviews. You never know what it might lead to. Once I did just this, and it resulted in me being hired to do a podcast for Ladybird Books.

Why not devise a standard reply you can send in response to press releases? Save it as a keyboard shortcut, so it takes only a few seconds to respond.

Try to be original, think of how to tell the story in a different way. I still want my content to be interesting, even if it is for a brand campaign. Try to make the content personal. Don't just take the money and post the link, think how you can add value with the post. The link will be clicked by more people if your post is interesting or useful.

A note of caution when working with brands, make sure it's worth it to YOU. You must decide your own fees and whether you're going to have a minimum product value for reviews. Whatever your limits are, just make sure it's worth your time. It will take time to test a product, photograph it, edit the photos, write up the review and promote on social media.

Ensure what you get in return covers your time. You can also ask other bloggers for advice. Blogging is such a helpful and supportive community, so, if you need help, ask another blogger. Email them, message them or join one of the many Facebook groups for bloggers.

Don't work for free, unless <u>YOU</u> want to, not because you're made to feel as if you should. The offer of high res images or perhaps they have written a wonderful post that you can use for 'free'… Doesn't mean you SHOULD post it. It's your blog, know your worth and you should post only what you want to.

Make it easy for PRs to work with you. Having a search bar on your blog makes it easy for them to quickly find out if you've worked with a particular brand before. Include an email address, no contact form as these can sometimes be off putting and have your social media links on the front page in a prominent position. Include a picture of you on your sidebar (not your dog or your baby!).

If you're an ambassador for a brand, it might be helpful to put badge in your sidebar. That way they can avoid any conflict with competing brands. A 'Work With Me' page can be a great place to summarise the brands you have worked with, how you work with brands and any other relevant details.

Keep in contact with brands/PRs you have worked with. Every month to two months, give all your PR contacts a quick email. Remind them of you and your blog and ask if they have any suitable opportunities on the horizon. Be confident and pitch to them. Confidence does come with a bit of experience. However, if you want to be successful, you need to give the impression of confidence to brands. If you want to work with a particular brand, then pitch to them. Don't wait until they come to you. Chances are they might never come across your blog.

A prime example of this in my life is my past collaboration with Diet Chef. I wanted to work with a weight loss brand and so I pitched to them. I laid out why I would be a great person to work with their brand. Why it would be good for them and what exactly I could offer them in return. This resulted in a six-month collaboration, which was the longest collaboration with a blogger that they had ever done.

Fancy pitching to a brand?

Write down your five favourite brands. If you can't think of any brands then grab your notepad and have a wander round your house. Look at the brand names on the products you use regularly and that you love. Make a note of clothing labels, kitchen equipment; all the brands you're a fan of. This part is important as you want to pitch to brands you actually like. That way if your pitch is successful the collaboration will be authentic. Discount any brands that don't fit with your blog.

Now transform into Miss Marple and do some detective work. You need to find the right person to contact, the person in charge of *blogger outreach*. If you can't find that person *PR/press* would be a good start. From here you can look through the press information and you might find the name of the person on a press release or other coverage the brand has received.

Once you have found them make sure you are following them on their main social channels. Now you're going to start to get their attention. Craft an authentic tweet about their product/service and tag them. This is a great way of putting yourself on their radar. If they follow you, you will be able to direct message them and ask for the name/email of the person dealing with blogger outreach.

Time to gather your intel. Check out the brand's social profiles and feeds to see what they're currently promoting. This is going to help you figure out whether your pitch is going to be well received and fit in with their brand's current campaigns. Remember brands are going to be planning ahead, so it's important to get your seasonal pitches to the brands in good time.

The ideal pitch is concise, professional, clear and intriguing. Attach your media kit and ask if they would like you to send a more detailed proposal. Then send it!

Get it done and move on. Remember, you might have to send ten pitches to even get one acknowledgement. Don't take this personally. Just keep trying.

You might be the type of person who would love a longer-term collaboration. In which case, brand ambassador programmes might interest you.

During my blogging career, I've had the pleasure of being a brand ambassador for many national and international brands. A brand ambassador acts as a representative for the brand to the public. There's no one magic thing you can do in order to become a brand ambassador, but there are lots of things you can do to put yourself in the best possible position.

Most importantly, write about the things you love, in your voice and be authentic. You want people and brands to identify with the real you and you want to secure a partnership with a brand that's a good fit and that you will enjoy working with, so there's no point in not showing the real you.

Brands like working with people who are passionate about things they love and who can then shout about their brand in the same way. Sharing your passions and creating exciting content will stand you in good stead.

Think of showing brands what you can do with every post you write, even if it's not sponsored. Use your posts to show your skills, whether it's lovely photos, brilliant writing or creative ideas, every time you write a post you have a chance to show off.

This should go without saying, but every time you deal with a brand be professional, deliver on your agreements and take pride in doing the best job you can. Every business you deal with could potentially want a brand ambassador in the future, so make your interactions count. Don't get drawn into any negativity on social media and don't moan. No-one likes a moaner and brands certainly don't want to work with someone who moans in every post.

What they do want is a reliable brand representative and someone who can project a consistent message. If you post every day for a week and then not for a month, the brand may think that's how you will represent them too and will be put off. Also, be consistent in your message and in your voice and tone, so you keep your authenticity intact.

Building your social media following takes time, but a large and engaged following is what brands would love from their brand ambassadors. As we discussed earlier the key is engagement though. Interact on social media, comment on other blogs and then people will comment on yours too. This engagement is really appealing from brands and is one of the major pulls that us bloggers have over more traditional advertising.

Remember working with every brand under the sun, might appear a little disingenuous to a brand who are looking for a long-term relationship. It's really flattering to be approached and asked if you would like to become a brand ambassador. However, you need to make sure it is the right move for you before you accept.

Do you love the brand? It will be hard work to promote a brand that you don't love. Is the deal exclusive? If it is, then you need to ensure you are not cutting out potential lucrative future opportunities.

What do they want from you? What social media coverage are they seeking? Do you have to attend an event? Will they cover your travel if they expect you to be there? What do you receive in return? Is there a fee or payment for goods? Is it worth it for the number of posts they expect? Is the brand a good fit for you and do you get enough in return for your promotion of their business? These are all great questions to help you decide if the opportunity is a good fit for you.

ABY'S ACTION STEP

I want you to create a hit list of all the brands you'd love to work with. Don't censor yourself, go crazy. It will be useful as you start pitching to have this hit list to refer to, so you don't lose time thinking about who to approach each time you want to pitch.

CHAPTER 28

Don't put all your eggs in one basket.

Many people share the same dream. To make money from their blog. Maybe even make enough to be able to give up the day job and work on their blog full-time. When you start trying to monetise your blog is can be a little overwhelming. Which option is best for you and your blog? Which will pay better? How do you know if an option is worth pursuing or even if it's a genuine opportunity?

As discussed, working with brands is very popular within blogging, but have you ever heard the saying, don't put all your eggs in one basket? I'm sure you have, it's a saying that most of us have been aware of for most of our lives. Yet, as bloggers, most of us do exactly that. We put most of our eggs in one, maybe two baskets, and hope for the best.

The digital world is amazing, and it can literally change your life, but it's fast-paced nature can lead to huge rapid changes. Changes which could ultimately affect the 'one-basketers' out there! For example, when Pinterest stopped allowing affiliate links on pins, this had a huge impact on the bloggers who used these as their primary income stream.

What if your income comes from coaching clients who come via your blog Facebook page. When there is an algorithm change and your posts get shown to less people, you could be in trouble. Your income declines as a consequence, possibly leaving you in a pickle financially.

This is why you should you have multiple income streams. It makes sense to have more than one revenue stream, not to spread ourselves too thinly, but to have income coming from multiple sources to support us if one of our streams dries up.

When people talk about revenue streams it can seem a little too business-focused for a lot of us more creative entrepreneurs. A revenue or income stream is simply a channel through which you make money from your blog.

Have I convinced you? OK! If you already have more than one stream, the first thing you should do is to investigate where your blog money comes from now. Then start to track this income. Do you make money through Amazon or another affiliate scheme? Write it all down and keep track of how much money comes from each stream.

Think about how you can add extra streams to your blog. I think having four streams, each bringing in 25% of your income would be ideal. This way if one dries up, you still have 75% of your income to support yourself and your family.

There are so many ways you can hustle to create multiple streams of income for your blog. As mentioned the main streams most bloggers consider are working with brands on sponsored content, accepting paid guest posts or taking on an ambassadorship. These are all great, and definitely a staple way to earn money, but how about adding in your own products.

This is where those info products come in. Maybe you're great at design and could sell a template that would be useful and solve a problem for your readers. People are always looking for ways to make their lives easier, so do just that with the product you create. You might feel you have a lot to offer your readers in a certain area, in which case you could consider writing an e-book or perhaps creating a course to package up your knowledge into bite-sized chunks.

If you have the skill to create a physical product, you could always sell your wares via a shop on your blog. Otherwise, you can always create a shop filled with products that are drop-shipped to the customer (meaning you never have to deal with the packaging/stock levels, etc.).

Maybe you're a wonderful photographer, in which case you could start to sell your images via a third-party site, or even take lots of wonderful stock images, which you bundle up and sell on your site. Taking this one step further you could create a paid-for resource vault on your blog to which you upload your wonderful stock images and charge a monthly fee for access.

Affiliate links are also a popular way to earn as a blogger. There are various ways which you can earn money via affiliate links, but I would recommend seeking those which pay you a percentage based on the purchases driven by your blog.

So, if someone clicks an affiliate link placed on your site and buys the product you receive a percentage of that sale. This way is preferable for new bloggers who might not have enough traffic to make the alternative pay-per-click affiliate schemes worthwhile.

However, instead of solely relying on schemes that pay out a small percentage. Look at the products and services you use personally to see if they have affiliate schemes. These often pay out much more to their affiliates and it's always easier to recommend a product you love and use regularly.

Just like sponsored posts, some brands will pay bloggers to promote their offers on the blogger's social media accounts. You might highlight the brand on Twitter, Facebook or Instagram for an agreed fee.

These are just a few ways to think outside the box in order to make sure your blog biz has a rock-solid income from multiple streams.

ABY'S ACTION STEP

Write down the current ways you make money from your blog. The think of which other income streams you can add to your business. Which makes more sense to you?

Hitting a plateau

There will probably be a few occasions in your blogging journey when you feel like your growth has stalled. You might have been blogging for a while, and yet you aren't seeing the visitor numbers you had hoped for. Your blog isn't growing as you had imagined it would.

This can be really disheartening to invest lots of time and effort into your blog and not see the return on this time, in terms of visitor numbers. There are a few common reasons which could be causing this lack of growth.

Your blog is too much about you. In the most part, people want information. They want answers to their questions; they want information that will help them to improve their own lives or businesses.

While internet 'friends' might be interested in personal posts, the rest of the internet community isn't as interested in these topics. If you can write posts which provide content that focuses on the challenges and pain points experienced by your readers, your blog will grow much quicker. Sharing your expertise and producing highly valuable content is the key.

Your content is difficult to read, with an unattractive layout. As harsh as it seems, people will only read your posts if they are laid out, attractive and easy to read. Huge blocks of text are so off-putting to the reader. This will prevent people engaging with your content. You can improve your posts readability by keeping your paragraphs short and by using headings, bullet points and images to break the content into manageable chunks.

People can't share it. I see so many people who aren't maximising the potential of their great content. Mainly because they don't make it easy for people to share it with others. It's vital to include social sharing buttons on your posts and make sure they work! Add in your Twitter handle to the Twitter sharing, so you're tagged in the share. If you don't, people will be MUCH less likely to share your post.

There's no incentive for your readers to return. For most blogs, the percentage of returning readers will be lower than the percentage of first time readers. You need to try to encourage people to return and the best way to do that is to get them to sign up to your email list, as I outlined earlier.

Maybe you're running too many ads. I realise that some bloggers make good money from ads. However, for me and many other readers, too many ads detracts from your content. They can interrupt a posts flow if they are within the posts. They can also remove the white space which is there on the page to give your content room to breathe.

Personally, I would rather keep people on my site for longer and have them more likely to return, than earn a few pounds from an advert. Obviously, discreet ads are preferable, but all ads should be placed on your blog with consideration as to how they will affect the user experience.

ABY'S ACTION STEP

Do you have any issues to resolve with your site, which could be limiting your growth?

How else can you boost traffic?

Most people who run an online business will say their biggest struggle is that they *'need to get more traffic.'* You need traffic to build your email list, you need traffic to sell your products, you need traffic to fill your courses. That leaves the big question — where do you get *'more traffic'* from? Yes, you could invest in lots of ads, however, that can be expensive if you get your targeting wrong. You could focus your time and energy on stellar search engine optimisation, but this can take time to produce its full effects.

So, it's a good thing you have other options.

Let's go back to guest posting for a minute. Being a guest on someone else's platform is a great way to get more traffic. We all need content. It's the one thing that remains consistent among all content creators—there's never enough. This is where you can help. By guest posting on other bloggers' blogs, you can in effect "borrow" some of their traffic.

To get this strategy right you don't want to simply regurgitate all of your old content and send it to lots of places all at the same time. In order to get the best results, you'll really need to create content designed with your host's unique audience in mind.

If you don't have a big email list yet, you can 'borrow' someone else's list to kickstart the growth of your own by scheduling a free event with a partner. As the person with the small list, you would create a compelling, free training course and set up all of the tech. Your co-host would bring their traffic. It's a great solution for both parties. You gain the extra traffic, while your co-host gets free content for their audience.

Being interviewed on someone else's podcast, YouTube channel, local events, industry conferences, an online summit, or on a blog is a wonderful way to get instant exposure to lots of new people. There are plenty of opportunities out there for creators in every niche to be featured in these ways.

You can kickstart your audience growth simply by making yourself available for these and other opportunities. Every time you feature on someone else's platform. Whether that's a blog, podcast or webinar you're getting a chance to get in front of an entirely new audience and getting a chance to grow your own.

CHAPTER 29

Getting more for less.

As bloggers we write posts, but is the continual production of brand new posts necessary or even the best way to promote and grow your business? What would you say if I told you that you could write less, be creative and possibly even reach new audiences? Sound good? I think so!

There can be quite a pressure to continue to produce new and useful content for our readers, but I think many of us are missing a trick. Just because you have written and published a post about, let's say, how to grow your Twitter following, this doesn't mean that everyone who read that post the first time is the ultimate audience for that particular post. Some people may have missed it, some people maybe weren't ready to learn the information first time round. Some people may like to listen to information when they are on the school run. Others might like something concrete to print out to assist their learning.

Don't waste time continually creating new content, when you haven't got all you can, in terms of growth, from that great evergreen post you created. You will find that a lot of your posts have a useful life after they first appear on your blog.

'You don't have to create content day in and day out. You just have to work on getting the content you already have in the hands of more people.' - Derek Halpern of Social Triggers

First, you need to find your highest quality evergreen content. You may know which your best performing posts are, or you may need to check your analytics. Make sure you're looking for the older posts that are still high in your top performing posts.

Now, how can you make them work harder for you? Could you extend your initial ideas and add anything to the conversation to enable you to write the sequel to your well performing initial post? If your evergreen post was a list, could you expand your individual points into a post each to create a series of posts?

Another option could create a webinar based on the ideas from the post and get interaction from the audience to delve deeper into the information in the post.

Facebook LOVES its own Facebook Live video, so why not create a shortened version of your post and use it as a script for a Facebook Live video? Facebook will do the work for you and show it to lots of people, so why not cash in on this while they are pushing these live videos so much.

If your evergreen post is part of a series of posts that fit together, maybe there is some scope to use them as the basis of an e-book. You can use plugins such as Beacon to help you turn your blog posts into e-books. This could then be sold on your site.

Maybe re-format the post or use it as the basis to create a useful printable. For example, if you had written about growing your Twitter following, you might choose to create a checklist to help people grow theirs.

Creating a Pinterest Instructographic could be an innovative way to repurpose. You create an infographics, but giving details on the steps to complete a particular project. Then you leave off the last few steps and ask the readers to click the link through to your blog to find out how to complete the task.

You can simply update an old post and republish. Keep the old URL for SEO reasons (unless you set up a 301 redirect), but add to it, format it, improve the SEO, change the image, add a better pin, a content upgrade and then republish it.

Go through your post and extract the most powerful points. Then use these points as Facebook content.

Perhaps linking back to the post or maybe just adding value to your readers without linking. Moving to Twitter content. This time you want to be looking for a click to tweet type quote of succinct few words that get your point across.

Examine the post and break it up to create an email series. Again, this could the basis of an opt-in freebie or even a paid for course depending on the content you have to work with.

Another great repurposing trick is to turn your post into presentation slides and upload to SlideShare, thus reaching a whole new audience. Then use the slides you have just created as the basis of a YouTube video. Add your audio as you talk through the slides and then upload. Then take it a step further and strip the audio from your YouTube video and use it as a podcast or an audio download.

Turn your slides into an infographic, using sites such as Piktochart or Visually. Then add this to the original post and use it as a pin on Pinterest.

Another idea would be to take an archived post, re-structure and update it, then use it as a guest post on someone else's blog. Obviously with a link back to your blog.

Simply re-sharing it would be another way to get more mileage from the content. I've lost count of the amount of people who say they share their posts a couple of times when they are first published and then they don't bother again!

Seriously, if you fall into this category you are missing a trick! How do you know your audience saw your two tweets, maybe they were working or sleeping when you tweeted it out. You're relying on people to go to your blog to seek out the post and a lot of the time people don't have time for this. You need to take your content to them via promotion.

I urge you to set up some automated tweets. This will do all the hard work for you and you can simply add the tweet in once and then forget about it. This will mean that when your potential readers are scrolling through their feeds they will see your content and will click on your links. Don't rely on them remembering you and coming to your blog to check whether you have a new post or not.

As well as saving you time and getting more people to see your content there are also additional bonuses for repurposing, such as a boost in SEO, reinforcing your message and also increasing your perceived authority on the subject.

Repurposing is a wonderful way to use content you have already created to attract more readers, spread your message and save yourself time in the process.

CHAPTER 30

Let's scale this baby!

There comes a time in our blog lives when we realise we can't climb the mountain alone…

I'd like to introduce you to Sally. Sally started her blog to preserve her young family's memories. Over the last few years her blog has grown, and she now earns a regular income from what still is her passion. Sally loves her blog, but she has concerns over the future of this blog she adores so much. Sally's concerns stem from the fact that Sally is knackered.

For the last few years Sally has been all things to all people and while she can just about stay afloat, she knows it isn't a sustainable way of life.

Sally's passions and dreams are being stilted. She does ALL the work in her business. She writes every word, takes every picture, edits every post, schedules every piece of content. Sally responds to every comment, even 'great post' and she tries to be EVERYWHERE, ALL the time, ALL on her own. Mainly, because she thinks she has no choice.

Sally used to love reading books, she would have considered it a passion. However, since she started her blog she's barely read one book cover to cover. In life before her blog, she had been known to read a book in a day. She misses reading for the sake of reading.

She dreams of creating a product line as an off-shoot to her blog and is saddened by the realisation that she will probably never find the time to do this either.

Sally never looks after Sally. She's constantly glued to her phone. Never feeling like she has time to disconnect from the nuts and bolts of her business. Yet, often at the end of the day, she feels unproductive. She doesn't seem to have time for those leisurely baths she used to enjoy so much. Rather now she jumps in the shower, so she can get to her laptop those precious few minutes earlier to make a start on that ever growing to do list.

She fondly remembers the time when a holiday was just that and it didn't matter if there was a poor internet connection. Hell, even none at all would have been fine! Now the thought of no internet makes her break out in a cold sweat.

Sally's business is running her (not the other way around). She's spending too much time working **in her business**, leaving no time at all to work **on her business**. She dreamed of a life which was far removed from the one she is living now. A life with more freedom and less grind. She wonders where she went wrong. Sally works every night and her thoughts are consumed by her ever-growing to-do list.

Sally never drops the ball, yet recently things have started to slip. She prides herself on her ability to nail the details. To be able to keep all the balls in the air, without missing a beat. Yet recently, if she's honest, she's missed a few beats, which has both worried and alarmed her. Was she losing her touch? Shall I tell you a secret? I was Sally. Are you a little bit Sally too?

Trying to do everything yourself within your business will and does take its toll. On your business, but also on you as a person. As we all know there are only so many hours in the day and with the many facets of blogging, it can often be impossible to fit everything in AND then find even more time to actually grow our businesses.

We often think we can't afford help, which leaves us doing the basic grind. Leaving us with zero available time to develop our businesses, to be creative or to enjoy ourselves. As quite simply, we're too exhausted to go beyond what we're doing to keep things ticking over.

Outsourcing even small tasks can make a huge difference. Even if you aren't ready to jump in feet first with a 'virtual assistant', using a site such a Fiverr or Upwork can hook you up with professionals who will do a huge range of tasks for such reasonable rates.

Think of the tasks you 'like doing less' in your blog. Not doing them would give you so much more time to do things in your blog that will make a much bigger difference. Things that will push your blog forward and allow you the scope to explore new avenues without running yourself into the ground.

You could even post in one of the many Facebook groups, that you need a certain job doing by a certain day and I'm sure you will find someone to do it for you.

It's important to think about the value of your time when you are trying to decide whether you can afford to outsource. The moral of this story is don't be like Sally; be smart and find people to help you grow your blog into what you know it can become.

So, you've come to the conclusion that you're a bit too much like Sally and you know you have too many balls in the air. You know you can't really continue going at your current rate and you're now convinced you need to find the perfect Virtual Assistant (VA) for you and you need to make it work. Let's face it, most of us don't have money to waste getting this stuff wrong.

Being clear on what you want and what you expect will set you and your VA up for a successful relationship. Start making a list of the tasks and programmes you'll need your VA to know how to do before you start to look for someone. You can then find exactly the right person for your needs.

Approach the process as the start of a partnership rather than an employer/employee relationship. Make sure you have put systems in place for a two-way communication to help develop your VA's feeling of ownership of their new position and to iron out any issues before they become larger. Ask your VA how they wish to communicate with you. What system is easier for them?

While it's sensible to pick someone who has complementary skills to your own, you need to know you will gel with them too. You will be working closely with your VA so this is crucial. I truly believe in hiring character and training skill and in my experience, this approach has served me very well in my own business.

Be clear about the budget you have and exactly what you need to be accomplished. You're already short of time, hence looking for a VA, so you don't want to waste time with people who are seeking double the fee that you are prepared to offer. Nothing has to be set in stone, but it's helpful to start attracting people in the right ball park initially.

You can always hire someone on the basis of a certain deliverable for a fixed fee. If you need to show the person how to do a task you can record your screen easily using software such a Camtasia or Jing.

Asking for recommendations can be one of the best ways to find a VA. Facebook is a wonderful place to connect with other people who might be able to offer you a personal recommendation. Giving a test project as a trial or for a one-off fee can be a great way to see if a potential VA will be a good fit and would be able to meet your needs.

Don't hold one bad experience against all future VAs. Sometimes things don't work out. Maybe a past VA hasn't done the best job for you; this is a shame, but it doesn't mean you will never find the right person for you. Learn, improve your handover/selection process and move on with an open mind. I've had three VAs that weren't a great fit for me, before I found my current (and amazing!) VA.

Make time for proper handover. Even before you start looking for someone, you can start building up a series of guides about how you do various tasks.

Then you will have them for all future VAs you work with. I suggest screen recording yourself doing the tasks you hope to outsource. The next time you're working on the tasks you will eventually hand over just record your screen. Over time you will build up a bank of videos, then when you hire someone their first task can be to watch the videos and create their own written processes for each task.

Set your goals and instructions clearly. Make sure you're both on the same page by detailing all of the expected tasks with a rough guide time for each. Having a super clear job description, which explains the specific details of the arrangement can be a great idea. You need to have a clear process for handing over work and systems that both parties are totally clear on.

It's inevitable that there will be some misunderstandings along the way and it's unrealistic to assume your VA (however well chosen) will perform tasks as you would do them yourself. However, it's important to be patient and give your VA time to settle into their new role. You won't regret it.

ABY'S ACTION STEP

Write down the tasks you do that you dislike? Which tasks take you lots of time, but don't yield a large financial reward? Add to this all the tasks that you complete that don't need your particular expertise.

Diversification Courses and Coaching

In September 2016, I decided to take my own advice and diversify my income streams even further. In order to help people more, I decided to start offering blogging courses. I wanted to be able to help people in a more through and effective way than I could in a post.

The idea of an e-course was born. The first topic on my hit list was productivity and I loved the idea of offering people a free five-day productivity challenge.

My daily workload prevented me getting started for a few months and then I decided to invest in some business coaching with Ceri from ThisWelshMother.co.uk. Ceri was fabulous, set me a target and within sixty hours the course was written. Ceri and I are now fast friends too, which makes me love the internet even more.

At this point in my journey, I'd mentored bloggers for free, done site overhauls, new designs and answered thousands of questions. I'd done all this because I genuinely love the blogging community and I like to play my part in helping it to grow, by helping the bloggers within it.

I come from a training and coaching background, so it seemed like the next logical step was to formalise the advice I offer so that more people are able to access it if they wish. So, I opened up coaching spots and blog critiques, to make sure my audience could access the help they needed to make their blogging dreams come true.

My free five-day productivity course launched and it has now seen hundreds of bloggers go through its doors and the feedback from this course has always been amazing. *'This course has, quite simply, been a game-changer for me. There are so many little bits of info in manageable chunks, along with challenges to help you achieve them' Carol*

'I've been blogging for almost 6 years but have been lacking motivation recently. I feel motivated and excited about my blog again and I'm determined to take it to the next level' Carolin

'I honestly couldn't thank Aby enough. So if you're looking for some focus and motivation to be productive with your blog then this course is for you'. Kelly-Anne

'I cannot explain the motivation and encouragement I've had from Aby on this course. I've got my focus back, set goals and it's encouraged me to move forward productively!' Fi

'It has given me the confidence to realise that I can succeed in growing my blog as a business. Aby has broken every part down to make it manageable and therefore achievable'.
Rachel

'Aby's 5-day productivity challenge has been like a shot of adrenaline, straight to the heart. I feel motivated, determined and BELIEVE I can succeed. Drive and hard work, not a problem, but Aby has shown me the how and why I was lacking. Her honest and simple coaching is a game changer. I've doubled my Twitter followers in 4 days'. Natalie.

'It's been a complete revelation. I know now what I need to do to get my blog out there more. Plus from my personal perspective To describe Aby things like big sister, BFF, teacher, coach come to mind' Markus

This amazing feedback from my first course spurred me to go on and create many more free challenges and paid courses. Of course, I continued to offer free advice through my blog in the form of my content, but these new offerings enabled me to help more people in a more structured way.

What they don't tell you about blogging.

There's no doubt that blogging is amazing. I've said it before, blogging has changed my life (hence, the title of this book!), totally, utterly and for the better.

For all the fabulous things blogging will bring into your life, it's a huge learning curve. Many of us started our blogs on a bit of a whim, having no clue where it would go or exactly what we were getting into. There's so much advice out there on how to blog better and you will even find a good amount of it on my own blogs, but there are some things you don't find out about until your feet are well and truly wet!

Your efforts will be rewarded, but it will take A LOT of work. Everything blog related takes time. That perfect blog post or Instagram image isn't just a fluke. Someone has spent ages taking the images, editing them, writing, proofing; it isn't a quick win. To post regularly and earn from your blog you will have to invest a serious number of hours.

You won't get rich quick from a blog. Starting a blog, building your followers and growing your online presence is a long road. Learning all the skills you need to become successful also takes time.

Blogging sucks you in and it's easy to get totally consumed by it. The online world never sleeps and there's always so much to do, that it can be difficult to draw a line. This is something I struggle with to this day if I'm honest.

You can do things your own way and still be successful. You should always do things your own way. You will shine if you do and people will respond to that much more than if you're trying to be a carbon copy of another blogger. It's easy to think that you should do everything others do, but if you're not feeling it, then don't do it. Simple.

It can make you feel amazing and awful in one single day. Hell, maybe even in one single hour! You can receive an email offering you the best opportunity, and twenty minutes later you find out your Tots ranking has dropped and you feel awful! There are a lot of ups and downs to blogging, thankfully many more ups.

You don't have to go it alone. Most people imagine bloggers to be working alone, but one of the best things about blogging is working with other bloggers. There is no doubt it's wonderful to be your own boss and organise your schedule, but it's equally awesome working with others.

You may end up with the best friends you ever had, who you met through blogging. I always used to think that people meeting online was a bit weird... Yet here I am with more 'proper' online friends than offline friends. Most have now crossed the line to be considered 'real' friends and the very best ones at that. We all spend hours online, I'm chatting with my blogging friends throughout the day and it's so lovely to have these friends who 'get' what blogging is and what it means.

If you build it, they may **not** come. Some people write a post and it goes down extremely well, resonates with lots of people and the traffic comes to their blog. This is not what happens to most people. Most people spend hours building their sites, more time writing fab posts and taking gorgeous photos, but this does not guarantee people will know about your blog and indeed pop over for a visit. You need to go and tell people your stuff is there and encourage them to pop by.

It does cost (something). I think there is a common misconception that all you need to blog is a computer and a Wi-Fi signal. While this is all you need to initially get going, there are various expenditures. Many people start on a free blogging site, such as WordPress. However, if you want to get a little more serious and potentially make money then you can't do it on a free site. You will need a domain name, a theme, monthly hosting. None of these things cost the earth, but they do cost. A camera, tripod, props, social media schedulers and monthly fees for access design programmes. All the little bits and bobs add up.

You're going to spend half your life on social media. A joy or a necessary evil, social media is very important to the success of your blog. There are so many accounts to manage, so many interactions to be part of and lots of promotion to do, all of which is very time consuming.

You need to develop skills. There's no doubt that good photographs will draw people to your blog, so you will need to improve your skills and you will also need to learn how to edit your pictures. As bloggers, we are all things to all people within our blogs. We need to wear many hats. You will find that you need to learn about SEO, possibly coding, accounts, the list goes on and on. Google will be your friend when delving into all of these areas for personal growth.

Blogging is competitive. Hundreds of people start blogs every day and even if you're good at what you do, there will be others who are good at it too. To be successful you need to work hard and have persistence, you have to be prepared for the knocks. Although it is competitive, it doesn't feel like it and on the whole, people are really thrilled to hear about the achievements of others.

Blogging is the most supportive place to be. It's the most wonderfully supportive place you can be, FACT.

There you have it, a few things they might not have told you before you started your blog. If you had been told, you would still do it right?! I know I would!

While I'm getting real, I want to share with you some myths about blogging that you should ignore immediately.

Myth #1. You need to be killing it on **every** social media platform. Social media can be all consuming. There are the old boys Facebook and Twitter, the cool kids Instagram and Pinterest, the young gun Snapchat and there's Steller, the weird kid that people don't really talk to, but would love if they did. Not to mention YouTube and Google+.

You could spend your whole life on all these platforms and you know what, there would be no guarantee that your blog would do any better than if you focused on only a couple. You would be consumed and probably burned out, trying to master them all.

My personal take is that you have to be on them all (although you won't find me on Snapchat, as it looks horrendous!), but you don't have to win them all. Find the platforms that you enjoy and that you know your audience likes too, maybe two or three and focus your efforts there, building your audience and having fun. Possibly auto posting on the other platforms that you are less enamoured with, so you have some presence.

Myth #2. You must be a fabulous writer to be successful. There's no doubt that the blogosphere contains some totally amazing writers, but you don't need to be the next JK Rowling to start a blog and for it to be successful. What you do need is a desire to achieve and the dedication to keep producing great content.

Myth #3. You need to post every day. OK, so in the past, I have posted multiple times a day. For the best part of three years, I posted on quite an insane schedule of between two-four posts a day, every day without fail. However, early on in 2017 I decided to stop, and I reduced my posting schedule dramatically. You know what happened? Nothing. No huge drop in traffic or other negative consequence. In fact, later in 2017, I hit #1 in the Tots100 ranking for the first time. So, I can assure you that posting daily is definitely not something you need for success.

Writing good quality (often longer posts) that are really useful to your audience, will have the same effect (better even) than posting shorter, less useful posts every day.

Myth #4. You need to spend mega bucks on a flash blog design. A beautifully designed blog with all the bells and whistles will no doubt make you look professional. Regardless of this, if your content sucks, people aren't going to stick around however pretty things look.

You can get a flexible theme so cheaply and there are so many tutorials around that will help you install it yourself. Spend some time on Canva or Picmonkey and you will be able to create your own header image, then BOOM your new design is up and running, looks professional and barely cost you anything.

Myth #5. Your blog is too niche. If you try to attract everyone you'll attract no-one. One major mistake I see lots of bloggers make is trying to speak to everyone. This is the wrong strategy. In actuality the more niche you are the more targeted your traffic will be and the more likely you will be to find the people who need to hear what you have to say.

Myth #6. You need sky high blog traffic to earn money. This really depends on which monetisation strategy you use. Low page views and certain advertising affiliations won't result in high earnings unless you combine it with another income stream such a sponsored content. However, if you have lower page views, but an engaged audience who you can positively influence, then brands will see this and you will be able to earn from brand collaborations. The engagement of the audience matters most for these kinds of monetisation strategies.

Myth #7. You must SEO all of your posts. It's unrealistic to think every post you write will be SEO gold. Sometimes you might just be updating your readers on something and these sorts of posts will be difficult to find a keyword for and it's probably pretty pointless in trying. Try no indexing these posts instead, so they won't negatively affect your SEO.

Myth #8. Blogging is easy and anyone could do it. Blogging is very time-consuming. Posts need planning, writing, promoting, pictures need taking, video need to be filmed, edited, uploaded and promoted, you need to keep on top of your emails, your blog maintenance, your brand work. The list of tasks is quite simply never ending. You need a lot of dedication and love for what you do to be one of the fewer people that continue blogging for more than two years.

Myth #9. Bloggers are blaggers. Some people start a blog because they want free stuff. The thing is it isn't free stuff as you trade off your time, expertise and exposure to your audience in return. I think they realise that eventually... If we're reviewing a holiday it's wonderful, but it's not the same as if we were just on holiday. Often I'm videoing and taking shots on my DSLR at the same time, add in some iPhone shots to share on social media, making sure you have taken everything in, while still staying present for your family is not a total walk in the park.

Most bloggers I know work very hard on their blogs and on behalf of the brands they work with. Often working full-time or running a house and looking after children, they're hustling, burning the midnight oil and are definitely NOT blaggers.

Taking the plunge

Thousands of people start blogs every day and blogging for a living is the dream for many of these people. If you've been blogging for a while, you might be working with brands and earning some income from your blog. How do you know when it's time to pack in the nine to five and *go pro?*

It seems lots of people have an issue with the title 'professional blogger'. I find this odd, as those same people probably wouldn't have an issue with the term professional footballer. It's the same thing, you are earning the majority of your income from blogging, as opposed to others who aren't. You're not better or worse than people who aren't professional, it's just two words.

How do you know when you are ready to take the plunge? You will already have a strong, confident voice. When people start blogging, they are finding their feet and so they might blog in different styles until they find out what feels right to them. After a while, this voice becomes more consistent and stronger as a result.

You'll have a community around your blog. People will be supporting you and your blog. Sharing your content and engaging with it. This means you have built a level of trust with your audience, which will be appealing to brands.

Brands contact you. At a certain point in your blogging career, brands and PR companies will start contacting you. For me, this happened as soon as I went self-hosted.

You want a more flexible blog theme. Are you frustrated with your theme? Do you long to alter your blog layout more than your current pre-made theme allows? This can be a sign that your dreams are growing and you need more flexibility to make them all come to fruition.

You've been blogging for a couple of years. As the majority of blogs are scrapped within a year, if you have stuck around for two years, this sends out a signal to brands that you are in it for the long haul.

You have a decent following. A large following isn't everything; better to have a small engaged audience than a bigger one that you can't influence. However, there's no denying that some brands will only work with bloggers who have a certain level of following.

Readers ask you for advice and feedback. If this is happening it's a sign they are considering you to be an influencer.

Earnings. You already make some income from your blog and believe this is scalable.

If the answer to these questions is yes and blogging for a living is something that drives you every day, then you may be ready to take the plunge.

Let's sum up what you'll need to succeed

Focus and determination. Why do you blog? To make it as a pro blogger you will need a clear reason, plenty of drive and a plan.

A strong voice. People won't want the read wishy-washy posts. You don't have to be controversial if that's not your thing. However, you need to have a strong personal voice. This helps readers to feel as if they know you and then they can identify with you.

Be an authority. What are you good at? What could you teach others? If you're a great photographer, then write about that with authority and confidence.

A strong brand identity. Is your brand instantly recognisable? Have you got the same images/artwork on all your networks?

You'll need to develop a routine. Any freelance lifestyle has a multitude of positives, together with some negatives. For some, it can be hard to get motivated and for others, it's difficult to clock off. Neither are great for you or your blog, so having boundaries and a routine is vital.

Hard work and a touch of obsession won't go a miss. I really believe that no-one becomes a full-time *pro* blogger without working really hard to get there. Countless late nights and days with very little time off are often a way of life on the road to becoming a pro blogger. I also believe that to continuously produce high quality posts each day, you need to be a bit obsessed with your blog.

A willingness to be vulnerable and authentic. The successful blogs are the one written by people who others can identify with and that are real. I believe that sooner or later people see through fakeness and so it's important to be yourself. Show you're a real human being just like them, not superwoman. A normal person working hard at something they love.

ABY'S ACTION STEP

What do you think you need to focus on before you take the plunge and go full time?

Can you make the shift?

As a psychology graduate, I totally believe in the power of our minds and you might find that in order to take your blog to the next level you need to shift your mindset.

So much of success is mindset. Successful people KNOW they will be successful, they don't doubt it and they work to make it happen. How do you develop the mindset of a winner?

Firstly, stop hiding and start being seen. No-one can ever work with you if they don't know that you exist! Yet so many bloggers and entrepreneurs are terrified of putting themselves out there. Honestly, I think more than 50% of people are sitting around paralysed forever and never wind up taking action.

Riddle me this: What's the worst case scenario? What are you so afraid of?

Let's be real here. Thousands of people will not flock to read your first blog post. But they never will if you don't publish the post. Don't be selfish! The longer you procrastinate, the longer your target market will have to wait for the solutions you have to offer them. You have value to contribute to the conversation and people who need what you have to offer are left waiting because you are procrastinating publishing a blog post, interacting in a Facebook group or attending that event.

Right now, stop being an employee and start being a boss. The big difference between an employee and a business owner is that business owners are visionaries. They create products and services, set boundaries, and make the rules. An employee is at the mercy of the boss. Wouldn't you rather be the boss? The great thing is your readers and clients WANT you to be in charge. That's why they're reading your content.

Stop treating your blog like a hobby and start treating is like a business. This shift might bring up some of your 'Imposter Syndrome.' We all struggle with this. Don't worry. If you're wondering, "Who am I to make money doing what I love?" You're not alone! What I want to remind you of is that you are starting a business for two reasons: (1) to make money and (2) to be of service. Those are the two goals of EVERY business. Freeloaders don't take your work seriously. It's in your clients' best interest that you charge a fair price for the work that you do.

Stop making stuff happen and start being prepared yet detached. When it comes down to it, you have no control over how many readers read your content. What you can do is prepare the hell out of your blog for a flood of readers. What would you need to do differently to satisfy a thousand new readers? Prepare your blog! And then let go of the outcome. Don't let it cause you anxiety. If something doesn't go as you planned or hoped, pivot and try something different.

CHAPTER 32

Keep on keeping on.

2017 round up

The Mamapreneur Revolution was created in September 2016 to be the home of my online courses. Since then it has gone from strength to strength.

2017 was a tricky year personally. We moved to France and it took so much time to even begin to settle in. In terms of my business 2017 has been a ground-breaking year. I attribute a lot of my business success in 2017 to certain things I focused on.

I focused on building an awesome community. There's no shortcut to this. You've got to keep showing up, keep giving value and have authenticity in EVERYTHING you do.

I posted a lot less. During the first half of the year, I had a hot seat with my mentors and they were shocked by how much content I was producing. I was publishing between two-four posts every single day and had been for years. My record was eighty-one posts in March once! They said what I already knew, but it's a leap of faith to stop doing something you have always done and hope that things improve. I was getting burned out and there was no way I would have been able to do that for another year. I now post around three times a week, but if I'm working with brands I may add a couple more in.

I focused on my building email list. As I shared, I was late to start growing my email list. I wish I'd known from the start that is was sooooo important. I focused on challenges and opt-ins and my list has quadrupled in 2017.

I stepped out of comfortable! A couple of years ago I decided I would stop letting fear stop me from taking hold of opportunities. 2017 saw me speaking on various stages (including Britmums Live), growing the Facebook live side of my business, launching our podcast, setting up my membership site and recording for various summits and podcasts for other people. One highlight was speaking at the Social Ads School online summit alongside huge names such as Kimra Luna, Melyssa Griffin, Amanda Bond and David Moazzez.

My membership community the Revolution Inner Circle, launched in July and I love it so much. The members are all amazing and I love being able to help them more closely. It's amazing to see all the wonderful things they are achieving.

I added products into my income stream. I love creating my own products which I can then sell over and over again. In addition to my three full courses, I have five free challenges, an evergreen webinar, and a workshop, plus spreadsheets, schedules, a roadmap and various workbooks.

I'm now focused on up levelling up my business and scaling during the next year. Focusing on our podcast (The Huddle), growing my new sites themamapreneurrevolution.com and abymoore.com, publishing this book, launching a successful summit, creating more digital products, growing my list and creating a new course and a new challenge. Just a few things then...

CHAPTER 33

Coming full circle.

13th November 2017

I sat on the Eurostar in Paris with mixed emotions. Part sad that I was leaving Ava for the best part of four days, part excited to be heading to what promised to be a wonderful event and to be spending time with one of the best friends I could wish for, Ceri. The final part of me was pretty exhausted, because well, I'm a mum!

After a day of travelling, I arrived at our apartment in London and immediately turned on the UK TV (purely to hear British voices) and popped the kettle on. Ceri was running late and so I settled in, then popped out to get supplies. After Ceri arrived we made our way to the QE2 Conference centre to register with hundreds of other Youpreneur attendees.

The excitement was already building. You could tell something special was about to happen. Goodie bags in hand we found the pub that was being used as a meeting place by other Youpreneurs.

Being introverts, we grabbed our wine and headed for the back of the room where we could chat. We had a wonderful night speaking to members of the event team (we kind of gate-crashed their works party!).

At one point, Ceri went to the bar and returned with white wine and Pat Flynn! To say I was shocked would have been an understatement. She had seen him at the bar, declared he was Pat Flynn (to him...) and then said he needed to come and meet her friend (which was me!). So, after chatting to Pat Flynn for a while, we headed back to our digs, full of excitement for the weekend to come.

To say Youpreneur was life-changing isn't too much of an exaggeration. We met our idols, we masterminded with them, gained validation from them. We made connections and started to believe in our ability to do more with our lives and our businesses.

The energy in the room was incredible. I felt inspired, I felt changed. I had a bigger vision and I started to believe it could happen. I could make it happen. Even after the first couple of sessions Ceri and I said if the event ended there and then we would have got our money's worth.

The following day was just as incredible as the first. We heard amazingly motivational stories and learned from the very best in the business. There were so many tears on the final day, but they were tears of utter amazement at the achievements of others and the power that we all have to change our lives and make things happen.

Since that Eurostar journey home I've really lived 'feel the fear and do it anyway'. I've pushed myself out there onto a bigger stage. Believed in myself more and valued what I have to offer the people in this world who need to hear what I have to say. There will always be people who know more than you, but *your* people need to hear it from *you*.

I wanted to help more mamas value what they do and help them build awesome businesses, that offer them the flexibility that I have found through mine.

The best way I thought to be able to do this on a bigger scale was the Blogging Changes Lives Summit, which I founded, and which had its inaugural event at the beginning of March 2018. I stepped out of 'comfortable', emailed industry experts and you know what? Some said yes. The power of just 'doing' is right there.

We also had the pleasure of having Chris Ducker on our podcast as a guest, which was mind-blowing and wonderful. We really set the bar high with our first guest.

Rewind to November 2017, the Youpreneur Summit had ended and I said farewell to Ceri. I headed off to the Eurostar. Little did I know the super stressful journey I was about to experience. Traffic jams everywhere meant I had to ditch the taxi and sprint (OK... walk very fast!) across London, dragging the heaviest case known to man! I reached St Pancras to find the check-in closed! I was so worried I would miss the train and then not get home to see Ava. Luckily, I managed to find some help and finally got through security with only seconds to spare.

I found my seat on the train, with my head spinning and full of possibilities, I pulled out my laptop and started to type with such conviction. The words came easily as if they were being fed through me.

By the time I reached France I was around three thousand words in. Three thousand words into writing this book. You CAN make your dreams come true.

Thank you for reading my story.

If you enjoyed reading my story I would love for you to pop over to Amazon and leave a review. It would mean the world to me.

23465952R00201

Printed in Great Britain
by Amazon